Betty Crocker
Bisquick
Impossibly
Easy Pies

Pies that Magically Bake Their Own Crust

WILEY

Wiley Publishing, Inc.

Published by Wiley Publishing, Inc., Hoboken, NJ

For general information on our other products and services or to obtain technical support please contact our Customer Care Department within the U.S. at 800-762-2974, outside the U.S. at 317-572-3993 or fax 317-572-4002.

Wiley also publishes its books in a variety of electronic formats. Some content that appears in print may not be available in electronic books.

Library of Congress Cataloging-in-Publication Data:

Crocker, Betty.
 Bisquick impossibly easy pies : pies that magically bake their own crust.— 1st ed.
  p. cm.
 ISBN 0-7645-5917-6 (hardcover concealed wire)
 1. Potpies. I. Title.
 TX693.C75 2004
 641.8'24—dc22

                                2004002262

Manufactured in China
10 9 8 7 6 5 4

GENERAL MILLS
Betty Crocker Kitchens

Director, Book and Online Publishing: Kim Walter

Manager, Cookbook Publishing: Lois L. Tlusty

Editor: Heidi Losleben

Recipe Development and Testing: Betty Crocker Kitchens

Food Stylists: Betty Crocker Kitchens

Photography and Food Styling: General Mills Photography Studios

WILEY PUBLISHING, INC.

Publisher: Natalie Chapman

Executive Editor: Anne Ficklen

Editor: Pamela Adler

Senior Production Editor: Jennifer Mazurkie

Cover Design: Jeff Faust

Book Design: Edwin Kuo

Interior Layout: Holly Wittenberg

Manufacturing Manager: Kevin Watt

Cover photo: Impossibly Easy Taco Pie, page 17

The Betty Crocker Kitchens seal guarantees success in your kitchen. Every recipe has been tested in America's Most Trusted Kitchens™ to meet our high standards of reliability, easy preparation and great taste.

FOR MORE GREAT IDEAS VISIT
BettyCrocker.com

Dear Friends,

If you love Bisquick Impossibly Easy Pies, you're not alone. Since the first Impossible Pie recipe was published back in 1978, it's been nearly impossible to keep up with consumer's requests for them. The popular pies, later renamed "Impossibly Easy," continue to be a favorite among Bisquick mix users more than two decades later.

And what's not to like? In addition to Bisquick mix, the pies call for basic ingredients such as milk, eggs, ground beef and shredded cheese—items you probably already have on hand. From classics like Impossibly Easy Cheeseburger Pie and Impossibly Easy French Apple Pie to tasty new combinations like Impossibly Easy Beef Steak Pie with Burgundy Gravy, this is the first cookbook ever to collect them all.

"Bisquick Makes the Impossible Possible," read the headline in *The Bisquick Banner*, a newsletter sent out to Bisquick Recipe Club members in 1981. A lofty claim, to be sure, but one Bisquick continues to make good on today.

Warmly,

Shirley Dolland

Shirley Dolland
from the Betty Crocker Test Kitchens

Contents

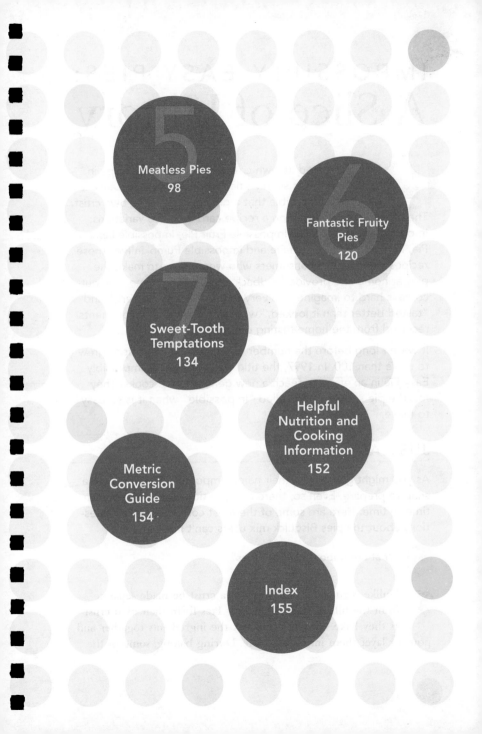

IMPOSSIBLY EASY PIES:
A Slice of History

Bisquick created its own crustless coconut pie recipe in 1978, and it was simply titled Impossible Pie because it didn't seem possible that a pie could make its own crust. The recipe was published on a recipe card with five variations: Impossible Chocolate Pie, Impossible Fruit Pie, Impossible Lemon Pie, Impossible Macaroon Pie and Impossible Pumpkin Pie. These recipes were sent to consumers who were asked to make the pies at home and provide feedback. "Interesting name. The outcome is hard to imagine," "a very quick and easy dessert," and "tasted better than it looked," were just a few of the comments received from the home-testing group.

It wasn't long before the number of Impossible Pie recipes grew to more than 100. In 1997, the title was changed to Impossibly Easy Pie in an effort to reach a new generation of cooks. They felt the pie shouldn't be called "impossible" when it is so easy to make.

JUST ASKING

As you might guess from their name, Impossibly Easy Pies are a snap to prepare. Even so, there are questions that pop up from time to time. Here are some of the most commonly asked questions about the pies Bisquick mix users can't live without.

Q: What are Impossibly Easy Pies?

A: Unlike regular pies that require a crust be made separate from the filling, Impossibly Easy Pies form their own crust as they bake. All you do is mix the ingredients together and pour or layer them into a pie plate. During baking, some of the

Bisquick mix sinks to the bottom and *voilà!*, a crustlike layer is created. A delicious filling, similar to a quiche or custard, bakes under a golden brown top crust. Impossibly Easy Pies can be main dishes or desserts.

Q: Can I double Impossibly Easy Pie recipes?

A: Yes. Just double the ingredients and bake in either two 9-inch pie plates or one 13 × 9-inch baking dish. You may need to increase the baking time slightly if you use the 13 × 9-inch baking dish. Be sure to check the doneness of the pie at the earliest time given in the original recipe. Look for 13 × 9-inch "Crowd-Size" variations included with many of the Impossibly Easy Pie recipes that follow.

Q: Can I substitute Reduced Fat Bisquick mix for Original Bisquick mix in recipes?

A: Because Reduced Fat Bisquick mix contains less fat, it may work differently in some recipes. To eliminate guess-work, about half of the Impossibly Easy Pie recipes in this book include kitchen-tested reduced-fat versions.

Q: Can Impossibly Easy Pies be made ahead?

A: Savory Impossibly Easy Pies may be covered and refrigerated up to 24 hours before baking. You may need to bake longer than the recipe directs—and watch for doneness carefully. Although premade pies taste equally as delicious as those baked immediately, they will have a slightly lower volume (refrigeration decreases the strength of the leavening). This is not recommended for sweet Impossibly Easy Pies.

Q: What's the best way to store a baked Impossibly Easy Pie?

A: Cool (if warm), cover and immediately refrigerate any remaining cooked pie. It will keep in the refrigerator for up to 3 days.

Q: Can I reheat leftover Impossibly Easy Pies?

A: If you're lucky enough to have leftovers, reheat them in the microwave. Place one slice on a microwavable plate, and cover with waxed paper. Microwave on Medium (50%) for 2 to 3 minutes or until hot.

Q: I'd like to make Impossibly Easy Pies for breakfast or brunch. Do you have any suggestions?

A: There are so many options to choose from, it's hard to narrow them down. Impossibly Easy Three-Cheese and Ham Pie (page 58), Impossibly Easy Bacon and Swiss Pie (page 74) and the aptly named Impossibly Easy Sausage Breakfast Pie (page 64) and Impossibly Easy Broccoli Brunch Pie (page 106) all are great breakfast and brunch choices.

TASTY TOPPINGS

Savory Pies

Avocado slices

Barbecue sauce

Chopped fresh herbs

Chopped/sliced onion

Chow mein noodles

Crumbled cooked bacon

Crushed cereals

Flavored mayonnaise

French-fried onions

Marinara sauce

Nacho cheese dip

Parmesan cheese

Pasta sauce

Process cheese sauce

Salad dressing

Salsa

Roasted red bell peppers

Shredded cheese

Shredded lettuce

Sour cream

Sliced olives

Sweet-and-sour sauce

Taco sauce

Tomato slices

Sweet Pies

Chocolate shavings

Chopped candy bars

Chopped nuts

Crushed cookies

Crushed granola

Fresh fruit

Fruit preserves

Ice cream

Ice cream syrups/toppings

Slivered almonds

Toffee bits

Whipped cream/frozen
whipped topping

Great Unbelievably Easy Menus

All-American Supper

Impossibly Easy Cheeseburger Pie, page 14
Corn on the Cob
Iceberg Lettuce Wedge with Thousand Island Dressing
Brownies with Vanilla Ice Cream
Milk

●●●●●●●●

Summer Dinner on the Deck

Impossibly Easy Triple-Cheese Pie, page 100
Three-Bean Salad
Watermelon Wedges
Peanut Butter Cookies
Lemonade

●●●●●●●●

Mexi-Meal

Tortilla Chips and Fresh Tomato Salsa
Impossibly Easy Taco Pie, page 17
Orange and Avocado Salad
Caramel Sundaes
Limeade and/or Margaritas

●●●●●●●●

Sunday Brunch

Impossibly Easy Sausage Breakfast Pie, page 64
Cantaloupe and Honeydew Melon Slices
Toasted English Muffins
Assorted Jams and Preserves
Orange Juice

Kids' Choice
Impossibly Easy Pizza Pie, page 72
Cherry-Banana Gelatin Salad
Carrot Sticks with Ranch Dressing
Rainbow Sherbet
Milk

●●●●●●●●

Thanksgiving
Roasted Turkey Breast
Mashed Potatoes with Gravy
Cranberry Sauce
Broccoli with Almonds
Dried Cranberry and Pistachio Salad with Vinaigrette Dressing
Whole Wheat Rolls with Butter
Impossibly Easy Pumpkin Pie, page 131
Impossibly Easy French Apple Pie, page 122
White Wine

●●●●●●●●

Special Occasion Dinner
Impossibly Easy Beef Steak Pie with Burgundy Gravy, page 28
Apple-Toasted Walnut Salad with Raspberry Vinaigrette
Crème Brûlée
Red Wine

●●●●●●●●

Appetizer Party
Crowd-size variations are great for entertaining.
Cut the pies into small bite-size squares.

Impossibly Easy Beef Stroganoff Pie, page 25
Impossibly Easy Bacon, Roasted Peppers and Feta Pie, page 77
Marinated Olives and Grilled Vegetables
Boiled Shrimp
Deviled Eggs
Smoked Salmon with Horseradish Sauce and Capers

1

Great Beef Ideas

⭐ = Favorite

Impossibly Easy
Cheeseburger Pie

(See photo insert)

Prep: 15 min   Bake: 25 min   Stand: 5 min

6 servings

1 pound lean
ground beef

1 large onion,
chopped (1 cup)

1/2 teaspoon salt

1/4 teaspoon pepper

1 cup shredded
Cheddar cheese
(4 ounces)

1/2 cup Original
Bisquick mix

1 cup milk

2 eggs

Cheeseburger
toppings, such as
ketchup, pickles
and mustard,
if desired

1 Heat oven to 400°. Spray pie plate, 9 × 1 1/4 inches, with cooking spray. Cook beef, onion, salt and pepper in 10-inch skillet over medium heat 8 to 10 minutes, stirring occasionally, until beef is brown; drain. Spread in pie plate. Sprinkle with cheese.

2 Stir Bisquick mix, milk and eggs in medium bowl with wire whisk or fork until blended. Pour into pie plate.

3 Bake about 25 minutes or until knife inserted in center comes out clean. Let stand 5 minutes before serving. Serve with cheeseburger toppings.

Reduced-Fat Impossibly Easy Cheeseburger Pie: Use Reduced Fat Bisquick mix and fat-free (skim) milk. Substitute 3 egg whites or 1/2 cup fat-free cholesterol-free egg product for the eggs and 3/4 cup shredded reduced-fat Cheddar or process American cheese (3 ounces) for the 1 cup cheese.

Crowd-Size Impossibly Easy Cheeseburger Pie: Double all ingredients. Spray 13 × 9 × 2-inch baking dish with cooking spray. Cook beef mixture in 12-inch skillet. Stir Bisquick mixture in large bowl. Bake 25 to 30 minutes.

1 SERVING: Calories 325 (Calories from Fat 190); Fat 21g (Saturated 10g); Cholesterol 135mg; Sodium 530mg; Carbohydrate 11g (Dietary Fiber 1g); Protein 23g • **% Daily Value:** Vitamin A 8%; Vitamin C 0%; Calcium 18%; Iron 10% • **Exchanges:** 1 Starch, 3 Medium-Fat Meat, 1/2 Fat • **Carbohydrate Choices:** 1

High Altitude (3500 to 6500 feet): Bake 30 to 35 minutes.

Impossibly Easy

Bacon
Cheeseburger Pie

Prep: 20 min Bake: **33 min** Stand: **5 min**

6 servings

1 pound lean
ground beef

1 medium onion,
chopped (1/2 cup)

1/4 teaspoon pepper

1 cup shredded
Cheddar or process
American cheese
(4 ounces)

1/2 cup Original
Bisquick mix

1 cup milk

2 eggs

1 medium tomato,
sliced

3 slices bacon,
crisply cooked
and crumbled

1 Heat oven to 400°. Spray pie plate, 9 × 1 1/4 inches, with cooking spray. Cook beef, onion and pepper in 10-inch skillet over medium heat 8 to 10 minutes, stirring occasionally, until beef is brown; drain. Spread in pie plate. Sprinkle with 1/2 cup of the cheese.

2 Stir Bisquick mix, milk and eggs in medium bowl with wire whisk or fork until blended. Pour into pie plate.

3 Bake 25 minutes. Top with tomato, remaining 1/2 cup cheese and the bacon. Bake 5 to 8 minutes longer or until knife inserted in center comes out clean. Let stand 5 minutes before serving.

Reduced-Fat Impossibly Easy Bacon Cheese-burger Pie: Use 1 cup shredded reduced-fat Cheddar or process American cheese (4 ounces), Reduced Fat Bisquick mix and fat-free (skim) milk. Substitute 3 egg whites or 1/2 cup fat-free cholesterol-free egg product for the eggs.

1 SERVING: Calories 340 (Calories from Fat 205); Fat 23g (Saturated 10g); Cholesterol 140mg; Sodium 390mg; Carbohydrate 11g (Dietary Fiber 1g); Protein 24g • **% Daily Value:** Vitamin A 12%; Vitamin C 4%; Calcium 18%; Iron 10% • **Exchanges:** 1/2 Starch, 1/2 Vegetable, 3 Medium-Fat Meat, 1 1/2 Fat • **Carbohydrate Choices:** 1

High Altitude (3500 to 6500 feet): Increase first bake time to 30 minutes.

Impossibly Easy

Lasagna Pie

(See photo insert)

Prep: **20 min**   Bake: **38 min**   Stand: **5 min**

6 servings

1 pound lean ground beef

1/2 cup thick-and-chunky tomato pasta sauce

1/3 cup ricotta cheese

3 tablespoons grated Parmesan cheese

1 tablespoon milk

1/2 teaspoon salt

1 cup shredded mozzarella cheese (4 ounces)

1/2 cup Original Bisquick mix

1 cup milk

2 eggs

Additional thick-and-chunky tomato pasta sauce, heated, if desired

1 Heat oven to 400°. Spray pie plate, 9 × 1 1/4 inches, with cooking spray. Cook beef in 10-inch skillet over medium heat 8 to 10 minutes, stirring occasionally, until brown; drain. Stir in pasta sauce; cook until thoroughly heated.

2 Mix ricotta cheese, Parmesan cheese, 1 tablespoon milk and the salt in small bowl. Spread half of the beef mixture in pie plate. Drop cheese mixture by spoonfuls onto beef mixture. Sprinkle with 1/2 cup of the mozzarella cheese. Top with remaining beef mixture.

3 Stir Bisquick mix, 1 cup milk and the eggs in medium bowl with wire whisk or fork until blended. Pour into pie plate.

4 Bake 30 to 35 minutes or until knife inserted in center comes out clean. Sprinkle with remaining 1/2 cup mozzarella cheese. Bake 2 to 3 minutes longer or until cheese is melted. Let stand 5 minutes before serving. Serve with additional heated pasta sauce.

1 SERVING: Calories 350 (Calories from Fat 190); Fat 21g (Saturated 9g); Cholesterol 135mg; Sodium 690mg; Carbohydrate 14g (Dietary Fiber 0g); Protein 26g • % **Daily Value:** Vitamin A 12%; Vitamin C 2%; Calcium 30%; Iron 10% • **Exchanges:** 1 Starch, 3 Medium-Fat Meat, 1 Fat • **Carbohydrate Choices:** 1

High Altitude (3500 to 6500 feet): Heat oven to 425°.

FAVORITE Impossibly Easy
Taco Pie

(See photo insert)

Prep: **10 min** Bake: **28 min** Stand: **5 min**

6 servings

1 pound lean
ground beef

1 medium onion,
chopped (1/2 cup)

1 envelope (1 1/4
ounces) taco
seasoning mix

1 can (4 1/2 ounces)
chopped green
chiles, drained

1/2 cup Original
Bisquick mix

1 cup milk

2 eggs

3/4 cup shredded
Monterey Jack or
Cheddar cheese
(3 ounces)

Salsa, if desired

Sour cream,
if desired

1 Heat oven to 400°. Spray pie plate,
9 × 1 1/4 inches, with cooking spray.
Cook beef and onion in 10-inch skillet
over medium heat 8 to 10 minutes,
stirring occasionally, until beef is brown;
drain. Stir in taco seasoning mix (dry).
Spread in pie plate. Top with chiles.

2 Stir Bisquick mix, milk and eggs in
medium bowl with wire whisk or fork
until blended. Pour into pie plate.

3 Bake about 25 minutes or until knife
inserted in center comes out clean.
Sprinkle with cheese. Bake 2 to 3 min-
utes longer or until cheese is melted.
Let stand 5 minutes before serving.
Serve with salsa and sour cream.

Reduced-Fat Impossibly Easy Taco Pie: Use
Reduced Fat Bisquick mix, fat-free (skim) milk
and shredded reduced-fat Monterey Jack
cheese. Substitute 3 egg whites or 1/2 cup fat-
free cholesterol-free egg product for the eggs.

1 SERVING: Calories 315 (Calories from Fat 170); Fat 19g (Saturated 8g); Cholesterol 130mg;
Sodium 540mg; Carbohydrate 14g (Dietary Fiber 1g); Protein 22g • % **Daily Value:** Vitamin A 18%;
Vitamin C 2%; Calcium 20%; Iron 12% • **Exchanges:** 1/2 Starch, 1/2 Other Carbohydrate, 3 Medium-Fat
Meat • **Carbohydrate Choices:** 1

High Altitude (3500 to 6500 feet): Increase first bake time to about 28 minutes.

Impossibly Easy
Mexican Fiesta Pie

Prep: **20 min**   Bake: **35 min**   Stand: **5 min**

6 servings

1 avocado, peeled
and sliced

1 pound lean
ground beef

1 medium onion,
chopped (1/2 cup)

1 envelope (1 1/4
ounces) taco
seasoning mix

1 can (4 1/2 ounces)
chopped green
chiles, drained

1/2 cup Original
Bisquick mix

1 cup milk

2 eggs

1 medium tomato,
sliced

1/2 cup shredded
Monterey Jack or
Cheddar cheese
(2 ounces)

Sour cream,
if desired

Chopped green
onion, if desired

1 Heat oven to 400°. Spray pie plate, 9 × 1 1/4 inches, with cooking spray. Arrange avocado slices in pie plate. Cook beef and onion in 10-inch skillet over medium heat 8 to 10 minutes, stirring occasionally, until beef is brown; drain. Stir in taco seasoning mix. Spoon into pie plate. Sprinkle with chiles.

2 Stir Bisquick mix, milk and eggs in medium bowl with wire whisk or fork until blended. Pour into pie plate.

3 Bake 25 minutes. Top with tomato slices; sprinkle with cheese. Bake 8 to 10 minutes longer or until knife inserted in center comes out clean. Let stand 5 minutes before serving. Garnish with sour cream and green onion.

Reduced-Fat Impossibly Easy Mexican Fiesta Pie: Use Reduced Fat Bisquick mix, fat-free (skim) milk and shredded reduced-fat Monterey Jack or Cheddar cheese. Substitute 3 egg whites or 1/2 cup fat-free cholesterol-free egg product for the eggs.

1 SERVING: Calories 360 (Calories from Fat 200); Fat 22g (Saturated 8g); Cholesterol 125mg; Sodium 600mg; Carbohydrate 18g (Dietary Fiber 3g); Protein 22g • **% Daily Value:** Vitamin A 24%; Vitamin C 14%; Calcium 18%; Iron 14% • **Exchanges:** 1 Starch, 1 Vegetable, 2 Medium-Fat Meat, 2 1/2 Fat • **Carbohydrate Choices:** 1

High Altitude (3500 to 6500 feet): No changes.

Impossibly Easy

Tamale Pie

Prep: **20 min** Bake: **35 min** Stand: **5 min**

6 servings

1 pound lean ground beef

1/4 cup chopped onion

1 envelope (1 1/4 ounces) taco seasoning mix

1 can (8 ounces) stewed tomatoes, drained and chopped

1/2 cup frozen whole kernel corn, thawed and drained

1/2 cup Original Bisquick mix

1/4 cup yellow cornmeal

1 cup milk

2 eggs

1 Heat oven to 400°. Spray pie plate, 9 × 1 1/4 inches, with cooking spray. Cook beef in 10-inch skillet over medium heat 8 to 10 minutes, stirring occasionally, until brown; drain. Stir in onion and taco seasoning mix. Spread in pie plate. Sprinkle with tomatoes and corn.

2 Stir remaining ingredients in medium bowl with wire whisk or fork until blended. Pour into pie plate, lifting ingredients to allow Bisquick mixture to flow into pie plate.

3 Bake 30 to 35 minutes or until knife inserted in center comes out clean. Let stand 5 minutes before serving.

Reduced-Fat Impossibly Easy Tamale Pie: Use Reduced-Fat Bisquick mix and fat-free (skim) milk. Substitute 3 egg whites or 1/2 cup fat-free cholesterol-free egg product for the eggs.

1 SERVING: Calories 305 (Calories from Fat 135); Fat 15g (Saturated 6g); Cholesterol 115mg; Sodium 560mg; Carbohydrate 22g (Dietary Fiber 2g); Protein 20g • **% Daily Value:** Vitamin A 18%; Vitamin C 6%; Calcium 10%; Iron 14% • **Exchanges:** 1 Starch, 1 Vegetable, 2 Medium-Fat Meat, 1 Fat • **Carbohydrate Choices:** 1 1/2

High Altitude (3500 to 6500 feet): Bake 35 to 40 minutes.

Impossibly Easy
Beef Enchilada Pie

Prep: **25 min** Bake: **35 min** Stand: **10 min**

6 servings

1 pound lean
ground beef

1 medium onion,
chopped (1/2 cup)

1 clove garlic,
finely chopped

1 teaspoon chili
powder

1/4 teaspoon dried
oregano leaves

1/4 teaspoon salt

1/4 teaspoon pepper

1/2 cup taco sauce

2/3 cup finely
crushed tortilla
chips

1 cup shredded
Cheddar cheese
(4 ounces)

1/2 cup Original
Bisquick mix

1 cup milk

2 eggs

1 Heat oven to 400°. Spray pie plate, 9 × 1 1/4 inches, with cooking spray. Cook beef, onion and garlic in 10-inch skillet over medium heat 8 to 10 minutes, stirring occasionally, until beef is brown; drain. Stir in chili powder, oregano, salt, pepper and 1/4 cup of the taco sauce. Sprinkle tortilla chips in pie plate; top with 1/2 cup of the cheese. Spread with beef mixture.

2 Stir Bisquick mix, milk and eggs in medium bowl with wire whisk or fork until blended. Pour into pie plate.

3 Bake 25 to 30 minutes or until knife inserted in center comes out clean. Spread remaining 1/4 cup taco sauce over top; sprinkle with remaining 1/2 cup cheese. Bake 3 to 5 minutes longer or until cheese is melted. Let stand 10 minutes before serving.

Reduced-Fat Impossibly Easy Beef Enchilada Pie: Use shredded reduced-fat Cheddar cheese, Reduced Fat Bisquick mix and fat-free (skim) milk. Substitute 3 egg whites or 1/2 cup fat-free cholesterol-free egg product for the eggs.

1 SERVING: Calories 370 (Calories from Fat 205); Fat 23g (Saturated 10g); Cholesterol 135mg; Sodium 580mg; Carbohydrate 17g (Dietary Fiber 1g); Protein 24g • **% Daily Value:** Vitamin A 12%; Vitamin C 4%; Calcium 18%; Iron 12% • **Exchanges:** 1 Starch, 3 Medium-Fat Meat, 1 1/2 Fat • **Carbohydrate Choices:** 1

High Altitude (3500 to 6500 feet): Increase first bake time to 30 to 35 minutes.

Impossibly Easy

Barbecue Beef Pie

Prep: 20 min Bake: 30 min

6 servings

1 pound lean
ground beef

1 small bell pepper,
chopped (1/2 cup)

1 medium onion,
chopped (1/2 cup)

1/3 cup barbecue
sauce

1 1/2 cups shredded
Cheddar cheese
(6 ounces)

1 cup Original
Bisquick mix

1 cup milk

2 eggs

Additional barbecue
sauce, heated,
if desired

1 Heat oven to 400°. Spray pie plate, 9 × 1 1/4 inches, with cooking spray. Cook beef, bell pepper and onion in 10-inch skillet over medium heat 8 to 10 minutes, stirring occasionally, until beef is brown; drain. Stir in 1/3 cup barbecue sauce. Spread in pie plate. Sprinkle with 3/4 cup of the cheese.

2 Stir Bisquick mix, milk and eggs in medium bowl with wire whisk or fork until blended. Pour into pie plate.

3 Bake 25 minutes. Sprinkle with remaining 3/4 cup cheese. Bake about 5 minutes longer or until knife inserted in center comes out clean. Serve with additional barbecue sauce.

1 SERVING: Calories 420 (Calories from Fat 235); Fat 26g (Saturated 12g); Cholesterol 145mg; Sodium 670mg; Carbohydrate 22g (Dietary Fiber 1g); Protein 26g • **% Daily Value:** Vitamin A 12%; Vitamin C 10%; Calcium 24%; Iron 14% • **Exchanges:** 1 Starch, 1 Vegetable, 3 High-Fat Meat • **Carbohydrate Choices:** 1 1/2

High Altitude (3500 to 6500 feet): No changes.

Impossibly Easy
Beef and Broccoli Pie

Prep: **25 min**   Bake: **35 min**   Stand: **5 min**

6 servings

1 pound lean
ground beef

1 medium onion,
chopped (1/2 cup)

1/2 teaspoon salt

1/4 teaspoon pepper

1 package (9 ounces)
frozen broccoli cuts,
thawed and drained

1 cup shredded
Cheddar cheese
(4 ounces)

1/2 cup Original
Bisquick mix

1 cup milk

2 eggs

Savory Topping
(below)

1 Heat oven to 400°. Spray pie plate, 9 × 1 1/4 inches, with cooking spray. Cook beef, onion, salt and pepper in 10-inch skillet over medium heat 8 to 10 minutes, stirring occasionally, until beef is brown; drain. Layer beef, broccoli and cheese in pie plate.

2 Stir Bisquick mix, milk and eggs in medium bowl with wire whisk or fork until blended. Pour into pie plate.

3 Bake 20 minutes. Meanwhile, make Savory Topping. Sprinkle topping over pie. Bake about 15 minutes longer or until knife inserted in center comes out clean. Let stand 5 minutes before serving.

Savory Topping

1/2 cup Bisquick mix

1/4 cup chopped
nuts

1/4 cup grated
Parmesan cheese

1 teaspoon dried
basil leaves, slightly
crumbled

2 tablespoons firm
butter or margarine

Stir together all ingredients except butter in small bowl. Cut in butter, using pastry blender or crisscrossing 2 knives, until crumbly.

Reduced-Fat Impossibly Easy Beef and Broccoli Pie: Use shredded reduced-fat Cheddar cheese, Reduced Fat Bisquick mix and fat-free (skim) milk. Substitute 3 egg whites or 1/2 cup fat-free cholesterol-free egg product for the eggs.

1 SERVING: Calories 465 (Calories from Fat 280); Fat 31g (Saturated 13g); Cholesterol 150mg; Sodium 790mg; Carbohydrate 19g (Dietary Fiber 2g); Protein 27g • % Daily Value: Vitamin A 26%; Vitamin C 14%; Calcium 28%; Iron 14% • Exchanges: 1 Starch, 1 Vegetable, 3 Medium-Fat Meat, 3 Fat • Carbohydrate Choices: 1

High Altitude (3500 to 6500 feet): No changes.

Impossibly Easy
Swiss-Beef Pie

Prep: **20 min** Bake: **30 min** Stand: **5 min**

6 servings

1 pound lean
ground beef

1/4 cup chopped
onion

1/4 cup chopped
ripe olives

1/4 cup chopped
green bell pepper

1/2 cup Original
Bisquick mix

1 cup milk

1/8 teaspoon
pepper

2 eggs

3/4 cup shredded
Swiss cheese
(3 ounces)

1 medium tomato,
cut into wedges

1 Heat oven to 400°. Spray pie plate, 9 × 1 1/4 inches, with cooking spray. Cook beef and onion in 10-inch skillet over medium heat 8 to 10 minutes, stirring occasionally, until beef is brown; drain. Spread in pie plate. Sprinkle with olives and bell pepper.

2 Stir Bisquick mix, milk, pepper and eggs in medium bowl with wire whisk or fork until blended. Pour into pie plate.

3 Bake 20 minutes. Sprinkle with cheese. Bake 8 to 10 minutes longer or until knife inserted in center comes out clean. Let stand 5 minutes before serving. Garnish with tomato wedges.

Reduced-Fat Impossibly Easy Swiss-Beef Pie: Use Reduced Fat Bisquick mix, fat-free (skim) milk and shredded reduced-fat Swiss cheese. Substitute 3 egg whites or 1/2 cup fat-free cholesterol-free egg product for the eggs.

1 SERVING: Calories 305 (Calories from Fat 170); Fat 19g (Saturated 8g); Cholesterol 130mg; Sodium 310mg; Carbohydrate 11g (Dietary Fiber 1g); Protein 22g • **% Daily Value:** Vitamin A 10%; Vitamin C 8%; Calcium 22%; Iron 12% • **Exchanges:** 1/2 Starch, 1/2 Vegetable, 3 Medium-Fat Meat, 1/2 Fat • **Carbohydrate Choices:** 1

High Altitude (3500 to 6500 feet): No changes.

Impossibly Easy
Chili Pie

Prep: **20 min**   Bake: **35 min**   Stand: **5 min**

6 servings

1 pound lean
ground beef

1 can (14 1/2 ounces)
whole tomatoes,
drained and cut up

1 medium onion,
chopped (1/2 cup)

1 envelope (1 1/4
ounces) chili
seasoning mix

1 can (2 1/4 ounces)
sliced ripe olives,
drained

1 cup shredded
Cheddar cheese
(4 ounces)

1/2 cup Original
Bisquick mix

1 cup milk

2 eggs

Sour cream,
if desired

Shredded lettuce,
if desired

Chopped tomatoes,
if desired

1 Heat oven to 400°. Spray pie plate, 9 × 1 1/4 inches, with cooking spray. Cook beef in 10-inch skillet over medium heat 8 to 10 minutes, stirring occasionally, until brown; drain. Stir in cut-up tomatoes, onion and chili seasoning mix. Spread in pie plate. Sprinkle with olives and cheese.

2 Stir Bisquick mix, milk and eggs in medium bowl with wire whisk or fork until blended. Pour into pie plate.

3 Bake 30 to 35 minutes or until knife inserted in center comes out clean. Let stand 5 minutes before serving. Serve with sour cream, lettuce and chopped tomatoes.

Reduced-Fat Impossibly Easy Chili Pie: Use shredded reduced-fat Cheddar cheese, Reduced Fat Bisquick mix and fat-free (skim) milk. Substitute 3 egg whites or 1/2 cup fat-free cholesterol-free egg product for the eggs. Serve with reduced-fat sour cream.

1 SERVING: Calories 370 (Calories from Fat 200); Fat 22g (Saturated 10g); Cholesterol 135mg; Sodium 770mg; Carbohydrate 18g (Dietary Fiber 2g); Protein 24g • **% Daily Value:** Vitamin A 24%; Vitamin C 10%; Calcium 22%; Iron 16% • **Exchanges:** 1 Starch, 1 Vegetable, 3 Medium-Fat Meat, 1 Fat • **Carbohydrate Choices:** 1

High Altitude (3500 to 6500 feet): Decrease milk to 2/3 cup.

Impossibly Easy
Beef Stroganoff Pie

Prep: **15 min** Bake: **35 min** Stand: **5 min**

6 servings

1 pound lean ground beef

1 jar (4 1/2 ounces) sliced mushrooms, drained

1 medium onion, chopped (1/2 cup)

1 clove garlic, finely chopped

1/2 cup Original Bisquick mix

1 cup milk

1/4 cup sour cream

1 teaspoon salt

1/4 teaspoon pepper

2 eggs

Chopped fresh parsley, if desired

1 Heat oven to 400°. Spray pie plate, 9 × 1 1/4 inches, with cooking spray. Cook beef, mushrooms, onion and garlic in 10-inch skillet over medium heat 8 to 10 minutes, stirring occasionally, until beef is brown; drain. Spread in pie plate.

2 Stir remaining ingredients except parsley in medium bowl with wire whisk or fork until blended. Pour into pie plate.

3 Bake 30 to 35 minutes or until knife inserted in center comes out clean. Let stand 5 minutes before serving. Garnish with parsley.

Reduced-Fat Impossibly Easy Beef Stroganoff Pie: Use Reduced Fat Bisquick mix, fat-free (skim) milk and reduced-fat sour cream. Substitute 3 egg whites or 1/2 cup fat-free cholesterol-free egg product for the eggs.

1 SERVING: Calories 275 (Calories from Fat 155); Fat 17g (Saturated 8g); Cholesterol 125mg; Sodium 710mg; Carbohydrate 11g (Dietary Fiber 1g); Protein 19g • **% Daily Value:** Vitamin A 6%; Vitamin C 0%; Calcium 10%; Iron 10% • **Exchanges:** 1/2 Starch, 1/2 Vegetable, 2 1/2 Medium-Fat Meat, 1 Fat • **Carbohydrate Choices:** 1

High Altitude (3500 to 6500 feet): No changes.

Impossibly Easy
Sloppy Joe Pie

Prep: **15 min**   Bake: **30 min**   Stand: **5 min**

6 servings

1 pound lean
ground beef

1/2 teaspoon salt

1/4 teaspoon pepper

1 medium onion,
finely chopped
(1/2 cup)

1/4 cup chopped
green bell pepper

3 tablespoons
ketchup

1/2 cup Original
Bisquick mix

1 cup milk

2 eggs

1 Heat oven to 400°. Spray pie plate, 9 × 1 1/4 inches, with cooking spray.

2 Cook beef, salt, pepper, onion and bell pepper in 10-inch skillet over medium heat 8 to 10 minutes, stirring occasionally, until beef is brown; drain. Stir in ketchup. Spread in pie plate.

3 Stir remaining ingredients in medium bowl with wire whisk or fork until blended. Pour into pie plate.

4 Bake 25 to 30 minutes or until knife inserted in center comes out clean. Let stand 5 minutes before serving. Top each serving with additional ketchup if desired.

1 **SERVING:** Calories 255 (Calories from Fat 135); Fat 15g (Saturated 6g); Cholesterol 115mg; Sodium 500mg; Carbohydrate 12g (Dietary Fiber 1g); Protein 18g • **% Daily Value:** Vitamin A 6%; Vitamin C 6%; Calcium 8%; Iron 10% • **Exchanges:** 1/2 Starch, 1 Vegetable, 2 Medium-Fat Meat, 1 Fat • **Carbohydrate Choices:** 1

High Altitude (3500 to 6500 feet): Bake 27 to 32 minutes.

Impossibly Easy
Steak and Tomato Pie

Prep: **15 min** Bake: **40 min** Stand: **5 min**

6 servings

1 tablespoon vegetable oil

3/4 pound beef sirloin steak, trimmed of fat and cut into thin strips

1/4 teaspoon garlic salt

1/8 teaspoon pepper

1 medium onion, finely chopped (1/2 cup)

1 medium stalk celery, thinly sliced (1/2 cup)

1 small tomato, seeded and chopped (1/2 cup)

3/4 cup shredded Swiss cheese (3 ounces)

1/2 cup Original Bisquick mix

3/4 cup milk

2 tablespoons butter or margarine, melted

2 eggs

1 Heat oven to 350°. Spray pie plate, 9 × 1 1/4 inches, with cooking spray.

2 Heat oil in 10-inch skillet over medium-high heat until hot. Cook beef, garlic salt and pepper in oil about 5 minutes, stirring occasionally, until beef is brown; drain liquid if necessary. Place beef in pie plate. Top with onion, celery, tomato and cheese.

3 Stir remaining ingredients in medium bowl with wire whisk or fork until blended. Pour into pie plate.

4 Bake 33 to 40 minutes or until knife inserted in center comes out clean. Let stand 5 minutes before serving.

Crowd-Size Impossibly Easy Steak and Tomato Pie: Double all ingredients. Spray 13 × 9 × 2-inch baking dish with cooking spray. Cook beef mixture in 12-inch skillet; drain liquid if necessary. Stir Bisquick mixture in large bowl. Bake as directed.

1 SERVING: Calories 270 (Calories from Fat 145); Fat 16g (Saturated 7g); Cholesterol 125mg; Sodium 310mg; Carbohydrate 11g (Dietary Fiber 1g); Protein 20g • **% Daily Value:** Vitamin A 12%; Vitamin C 4%; Calcium 20%; Iron 10% • **Exchanges:** 1/2 Starch, 1/2 Vegetable, 2 1/2 Medium-Fat Meat, 1/2 Fat • **Carbohydrate Choices:** 1

High Altitude (3500 to 6500 feet): Bake 38 to 43 minutes.

Impossibly Easy
Beef Steak Pie
with Burgundy Gravy

Prep: **15 min** Bake: **30 min**

6 servings

2 teaspoons
vegetable oil

1/2 pound beef
sirloin steak, trimmed
of fat and cut into
thin bite-size strips

1/2 medium onion,
cut into thin wedges

1/2 teaspoon garlic
salt

1/8 teaspoon pepper

1 jar (4 1/2 ounces)
sliced mushrooms,
drained

1/2 cup shredded
carrots (about
1 medium)

1/2 cup Original
Bisquick mix

1 cup milk

2 eggs

1 jar (10 to 12
ounces) beef gravy

3 tablespoons red
Burgundy wine or
beef broth

1 Heat oven to 400°. Spray pie plate, 9 × 1 1/4 inches, with cooking spray.

2 Heat oil in 10-inch skillet over medium-high heat until hot. Cook beef, onion, garlic salt and pepper in oil about 5 minutes, stirring occasionally, until beef is brown and onion is tender; drain if necessary.

3 Place beef mixture in pie plate. Top with mushrooms and carrots; mix slightly. Stir Bisquick mix, milk and eggs in medium bowl with wire whisk or fork until blended. Pour into pie plate.

4 Bake 25 to 30 minutes or until knife inserted in center comes out clean.

5 Meanwhile, heat gravy as directed on jar. Stir in wine. Spoon gravy over each serving.

1 SERVING: Calories 180 (Calories from Fat 70); Fat 8g (Saturated 3g); Cholesterol 95mg; Sodium 640mg; Carbohydrate 13g (Dietary Fiber 1g); Protein 14g • **% Daily Value:** Vitamin A 38%; Vitamin C 0%; Calcium 8%; Iron 10% • **Exchanges:** 1/2 Starch, 1 Vegetable, 1 1/2 Medium-Fat Meat, 1 Fat • **Carbohydrate Choices:** 1

High Altitude (3500 to 6500 feet): Use 2/3 cup Bisquick mix. Bake 30 to 35 minutes.

Impossibly Easy
Reuben Pie

Prep: **10 min** Bake: **35 min** Stand: **5 min**

6 servings

2 packages (2 1/2 ounces each) sliced corned beef, cut up, or 1 can (12 ounces) corned beef

1 can (8 ounces) sauerkraut, drained

1 cup shredded Swiss cheese (4 ounces)

3/4 cup Original Bisquick mix

1 cup milk

1/4 cup Thousand Island dressing

1/2 teaspoon caraway seed

2 eggs

1 Heat oven to 400°. Spray pie plate, 9 × 1 1/4 inches, with cooking spray. Stir together corned beef, sauerkraut and cheese in pie plate.

2 Stir remaining ingredients in medium bowl with wire whisk or fork until blended. Pour into pie plate, lifting ingredients to allow baking mix mixture to flow into pie plate.

3 Bake 30 to 35 minutes or until knife inserted in center comes out clean. Let stand 5 minutes before serving.

Reduced-Fat Impossibly Easy Reuben Pie: Use shredded reduced-fat Swiss cheese, Reduced Fat Bisquick mix, fat-free (skim) milk and reduced-fat Thousand Island dressing. Substitute 3 egg whites or 1/2 cup fat-free cholesterol-free egg product for the eggs.

1 SERVING: Calories 250 (Calories from Fat 135); Fat 15g (Saturated 6g); Cholesterol 105mg; Sodium 980mg; Carbohydrate 14g (Dietary Fiber 1g); Protein 15g • % Daily Value: Vitamin A 6%; Vitamin C 4%; Calcium 28%; Iron 8% • Exchanges: 1/2 Starch, 1 Vegetable, 2 Medium-Fat Meat, 1 Fat • Carbohydrate Choices: 1

High Altitude (3500 to 6500 feet): No changes.

Impossibly Easy
Philly Cheese Steak Pie

Prep: **15 min** Bake: **33 min**

6 servings

1/2 pound sliced cooked roast beef, cut into 1/2-inch strips

1 tablespoon vegetable oil

1 small onion, cut in half and thinly sliced

1/2 medium green bell pepper, thinly sliced

1/2 cup Original Bisquick mix

1 cup milk

2 eggs

3/4 cup cheese dip (from 15-ounce jar)

1. Heat oven to 400°. Spray pie plate, 9 × 1 1/4 inches, with cooking spray. Place beef in pie plate.

2. Heat oil in 10-inch skillet over medium heat until hot. Cook onion and bell pepper in oil 5 to 8 minutes, stirring occasionally, until tender. Place in pie plate.

3. Stir Bisquick mix, milk and eggs in medium bowl with wire whisk or fork until blended. Pour into pie plate.

4. Bake 28 to 33 minutes or until knife inserted in center comes out clean.

5. Meanwhile, place cheese dip in small microwavable bowl. Microwave uncovered on High 30 to 45 seconds or until warm; stir. Spoon about 2 tablespoons warm cheese dip over each serving.

1 SERVING: Calories 255 (Calories from Fat 145); Fat 16g (Saturated 6g); Cholesterol 115mg; Sodium 390mg; Carbohydrate 11g (Dietary Fiber 1g); Protein 17g • % **Daily Value:** Vitamin A 10%; Vitamin C 12%; Calcium 14%; Iron 10% • **Exchanges:** 1/2 Starch, 1/2 Vegetable, 2 Medium-Fat Meat, 1 Fat • **Carbohydrate Choices:** 1

High Altitude (3500 to 6500 feet): Use 2/3 cup Bisquick mix. Bake 33 to 38 minutes.

Impossibly Easy
Meatball Pie

Prep: 10 min **Bake: 30 min**

6 servings

1 package (16 ounces) frozen meatballs, thawed

1 cup shredded mozzarella cheese (4 ounces)

1/2 cup Original Bisquick mix

1 cup milk

2 eggs

3/4 cup tomato pasta sauce (any variety)

1 Heat oven to 400°. Spray pie plate, 9 × 1 1/4 inches, with cooking spray. Place meatballs in pie plate. Sprinkle with cheese.

2 Stir Bisquick mix, milk and eggs in medium bowl with wire whisk or fork until blended. Pour into pie plate.

3 Bake 25 to 30 minutes or until knife inserted in center comes out clean.

4 Meanwhile, cook pasta sauce until thoroughly heated. Spoon 2 table-spoons pasta sauce over each serving.

1 SERVING: Calories 390 (Calories from Fat 200); Fat 22g (Saturated 9g); Cholesterol 165mg; Sodium 880mg; Carbohydrate 23g (Dietary Fiber 1g); Protein 25g • **% Daily Value:** Vitamin A 12%; Vitamin C 4%; Calcium 26%; Iron 16% • **Exchanges:** 1 1/2 Starch, 4 Medium-Fat Meat, 1 Fat • **Carbohydrate Choices:** 1 1/2

High Altitude (3500 to 6500 feet): Bake 30 to 35 minutes.

2

Savory Chicken and Turkey Suppers

= Favorite

Impossibly Easy
Chicken
Primavera Pie

Prep: **15 min**   Bake: **35 min**   Stand: **5 min**

6 servings

1 1/2 cups cut-up cooked chicken

1 package (9 ounces) frozen asparagus cuts, thawed and well drained

1 cup frozen stir-fry bell peppers and onions (from 16-ounce bag), thawed and well drained

1/3 cup grated Parmesan cheese

1/2 cup Original Bisquick mix

1 cup milk

1/2 teaspoon salt

2 eggs

1 Heat oven to 400°. Spray pie plate, 9 × 1 1/4 inches, with cooking spray. Layer chicken, asparagus, stir-fry mixture and cheese in pie plate.

2 Stir remaining ingredients in medium bowl with wire whisk or fork until blended. Pour into pie plate.

3 Bake 30 to 35 minutes or until knife inserted in center comes out clean. Let stand 5 minutes before serving.

1 SERVING: Calories 260 (Calories from Fat 110); Fat 12g (Saturated 5g); Cholesterol 110mg; Sodium 720mg; Carbohydrate 17g (Dietary Fiber 1g); Protein 21g • % Daily Value: Vitamin A 18%; Vitamin C 10%; Calcium 30%; Iron 8% • Exchanges: 1 Starch, 3 Lean Meat, 1/2 Fat • Carbohydrate Choices: 1

High Altitude (3500 to 6500 feet): Bake 38 to 40 minutes.

Impossibly Easy
Italian Chicken Pie

Prep: **20 min** Bake: **43 min** Stand: **5 min**

6 servings

1 1/2 cups cut-up cooked chicken or turkey

1 1/4 cups shredded mozzarella cheese (5 ounces)

1/3 cup grated Parmesan cheese

1/2 teaspoon dried oregano leaves

1/2 teaspoon dried basil leaves

1/2 teaspoon garlic powder

1 can (8 ounces) tomato sauce

1/2 cup Original Bisquick mix

1 cup milk

1/4 teaspoon pepper

2 eggs

1 Heat oven to 400°. Spray pie plate, 9 × 1 1/4 inches, with cooking spray. Stir together chicken, 1/2 cup of the mozzarella cheese, the Parmesan cheese, oregano, basil, garlic powder and 1/2 cup of the tomato sauce in small bowl. Spoon into pie plate.

2 Stir Bisquick mix, milk, pepper and eggs in medium bowl with wire whisk or fork until blended. Pour into pie plate.

3 Bake 35 minutes. Sprinkle with remaining 3/4 cup mozzarella cheese. Bake 5 to 8 minutes longer or until knife inserted in center comes out clean. Let stand 5 minutes before serving. Serve with remaining tomato sauce, heated if desired.

Reduced-Fat Impossibly Easy Italian Chicken Pie: Use shredded part-skim mozzarella cheese, Reduced Fat Bisquick mix and fat-free (skim) milk. Substitute 3 egg whites or 1/2 cup fat-free cholesterol-free egg product for the eggs.

Crowd-Size Impossibly Easy Italian Chicken Pie: Double all ingredients. Spray 13 × 9 × 2-inch baking dish with cooking spray. Bake as directed.

1 SERVING: Calories 290 (Calories from Fat 110); Fat 12g (Saturated 6g); Cholesterol 120mg; Sodium 690mg; Carbohydrate 12g (Dietary Fiber 1g); Protein 23g • **% Daily Value:** Vitamin A 12%; Vitamin C 4%; Calcium 34%; Iron 8% • **Diet Exchanges:** 1 Starch, 3 Lean Meat, 1 Fat • **Carbohydrate Choices:** 1

High Altitude (3500 to 6500 feet): No changes.

Impossibly Easy
Chicken–Vegetable Pie

Prep: **20 min** Bake: **35 min** Stand: **5 min**

6 servings

1 cup cut-up cooked
chicken or turkey

1 small zucchini,
chopped (1 cup)

1 large tomato,
chopped (1 cup)

1 medium onion,
chopped (1/2 cup)

1/3 cup grated
Parmesan cheese

1/2 cup Original
Bisquick mix

1 cup milk

1/2 teaspoon salt

1/4 teaspoon pepper

2 eggs

Sliced tomato,
if desired

Sliced zucchini,
if desired

1 Heat oven to 400°. Spray pie plate, 9 × 1 1/4 inches, with cooking spray. Stir together chicken, chopped zucchini, chopped tomato, onion and cheese in medium bowl. Spoon evenly into pie plate.

2 Stir remaining ingredients in medium bowl with wire whisk or fork. Pour into pie plate.

3 Bake about 35 minutes or until knife inserted in center comes out clean. Let stand 5 minutes before serving. Garnish with sliced tomato and zucchini.

1 SERVING: Calories 170 (Calories from Fat 65); Fat 7g (Saturated 3g); Cholesterol 100mg; Sodium 510mg; Carbohydrate 12g (Dietary Fiber 1g); Protein 14g • **% Daily Value:** Vitamin A 12%; Vitamin C 6%; Calcium 16%; Iron 6% • **Exchanges:** 1/2 Starch, 1 Vegetable, 2 Lean Meat • **Carbohydrate Choices:** 1

High Altitude (3500 to 6500 feet): Use 10 × 1 1/2-inch pie plate.

Impossibly Easy
Chicken Taco Pie

Prep: **10 min** Bake: **37 min** Stand: **5 min**

6 servings

2 cups cut-up
cooked chicken

1 medium onion,
chopped (1/2 cup)

2 tablespoons
taco seasoning mix
(from 1 1/4-ounce
envelope)

1 cup Original
Bisquick mix

1 cup milk

2 eggs

1 cup shredded
Cheddar cheese
(4 ounces)

Shredded lettuce,
if desired

Chopped tomato,
if desired

Sour cream,
if desired

1 Heat oven to 400°. Spray pie plate, 9 × 1 1/4 inches, with cooking spray. Stir together chicken, onion and taco seasoning mix in medium bowl. Spread in pie plate.

2 Stir Bisquick mix, milk and eggs in medium bowl with wire whisk or fork until blended. Pour into pie plate.

3 Bake 30 to 35 minutes or until knife inserted in center comes out clean. Sprinkle with cheese. Bake 1 to 2 minutes longer or until cheese is melted. Let stand 5 minutes before serving. Serve with lettuce, tomato and sour cream.

Reduced-Fat Impossibly Easy Chicken Taco Pie: Use Reduced Fat Bisquick mix, fat-free (skim) milk and shredded reduced-fat Cheddar cheese. Substitute 3 egg whites or 1/2 cup fat-free cholesterol-free egg product for the eggs.

1 **SERVING:** Calories 305 (Calories from Fat 135); Fat 15g (Saturated 7g); Cholesterol 135mg; Sodium 640mg; Carbohydrate 19g (Dietary Fiber 1g); Protein 23g • % Daily Value: Vitamin A 14%; Vitamin C 2%; Calcium 20%; Iron 8% • **Exchanges:** 1 Starch, 3 Medium-Fat Meat • **Carbohydrate Choices:** 1

High Altitude (3500 to 6500 feet): Bake 35 to 40 minutes.

Impossibly Easy
Chicken Pot Pie

Prep: **15 min** Bake: **35 min** Stand: **5 min**

6 servings

2 cups cut-up cooked chicken or turkey

1 cup frozen peas and carrots, thawed and drained

1/4 cup sliced mushrooms

1/4 cup chopped onion

1/2 cup Original Bisquick mix

1 cup milk

1/2 teaspoon salt

1/8 teaspoon pepper

2 eggs

1 Heat oven to 400°. Spray pie plate, 9 × 1 1/4 inches, with cooking spray. Stir together chicken, peas and carrots, mushrooms and onion in pie plate.

2 Stir remaining ingredients in medium bowl with wire whisk or fork until blended. Pour into pie plate.

3 Bake 30 to 35 minutes or until knife inserted in center comes out clean. Let stand 5 minutes before serving.

Reduced-Fat Impossibly Easy Chicken Pot Pie: Use Reduced Fat Bisquick mix and fat-free (skim) milk. Substitute 3 egg whites or 1/2 cup fat-free cholesterol-free egg product for the eggs.

Impossibly Easy Tuna Pot Pie: Use 1 can (6 ounces) tuna, drained, instead of the chicken.

1 SERVING: Calories 185 (Calories from Fat 65); Fat 7g (Saturated 2g); Cholesterol 115mg; Sodium 440mg; Carbohydrate 12g (Dietary Fiber 1g); Protein 18g • **% Daily Value:** Vitamin A 54%; Vitamin C 2%; Calcium 8%; Iron 8% • **Exchanges:** 1 Starch, 2 Lean Meat • **Carbohydrate Choices:** 1

High Altitude (3500 to 6500 feet): Bake 33 to 38 minutes.

Impossibly Easy
Chicken–Pesto Pie

Prep: 15 min   Bake: 37 min   Stand: 5 min

6 servings

2 cups cut-up cooked chicken or turkey

1/2 cup diced red bell pepper

1/4 cup basil pesto

1 cup shredded mozzarella cheese (4 ounces)

1/2 cup Original Bisquick mix

1 cup milk

2 eggs

1 Heat oven to 400°. Spray pie plate, 9 × 1 1/4 inches, with cooking spray. Mix chicken, bell pepper and pesto in medium bowl. Spread in pie plate. Sprinkle 1/2 cup of the cheese over chicken mixture.

2 Stir Bisquick mix, milk and eggs in medium bowl with wire whisk or fork until blended. Pour into pie plate.

3 Bake 30 to 35 minutes or until knife inserted in center comes out clean. Sprinkle with remaining 1/2 cup cheese. Bake 1 to 2 minutes longer or until cheese is melted. Let stand 5 minutes before serving.

Crowd-Size Impossibly Easy Chicken-Pesto Pie: Double all ingredients. Spray 13 x 9 x 2-inch baking dish with cooking spray. Mix chicken mixture in large bowl. Stir Bisquick mixture in large bowl. Bake 31 to 38 minutes, then sprinkle with cheese and bake 2 to 3 minutes longer.

1 SERVING: Calories 275 (Calories from Fat 145); Fat 16g (Saturated 5g); Cholesterol 125mg; Sodium 410mg; Carbohydrate 10g (Dietary Fiber 1g); Protein 23g • % Daily Value: Vitamin A 22%; Vitamin C 20%; Calcium 26%; Iron 8% • Exchanges: 1/2 Starch, 3 Medium-Fat Meat • Carbohydrate Choices: 1/2

High Altitude (3500 to 6500 feet): Use 3/4 cup Bisquick mix.

Impossibly Easy
Chicken Tamale Pie

Prep: **15 min**   Bake: **35 min**   Stand: **5 min**

6 servings

1 cup cut-up cooked chicken or turkey

3/4 cup frozen whole kernel corn, thawed and drained

1 envelope (1 1/4 ounces) taco seasoning mix

1 can (4 1/2 ounces) chopped green chiles, drained

3/4 cup shredded Cheddar or Monterey Jack cheese (3 ounces)

1/2 cup Original Bisquick mix

1 cup milk

2 eggs

Sour cream, if desired

Shredded lettuce, if desired

1 Heat oven to 400°. Spray pie plate, 9 × 1 1/4 inches, with cooking spray. Stir together chicken, corn and taco seasoning mix in small bowl. Spread in pie plate. Sprinkle with chiles and cheese.

2 Stir Bisquick mix, milk and eggs in medium bowl with wire whisk or fork until blended. Pour into pie plate.

3 Bake about 35 minutes or until knife inserted in center comes out clean. Let stand 5 minutes before serving. Serve with sour cream and lettuce.

Reduced-Fat Impossibly Easy Chicken Tamale Pie: Use shredded reduced-fat Cheddar or Monterey Jack cheese, Reduced Fat Bisquick mix and fat-free (skim) milk. Substitute 3 egg whites or 1/2 cup fat-free cholesterol-free egg product for the eggs.

1 SERVING: Calories 230 (Calories from Fat 100); Fat 11g (Saturated 5g); Cholesterol 110mg; Sodium 620mg; Carbohydrate 17g (Dietary Fiber 2g); Protein 15g • **% Daily Value:** Vitamin A 20%; Vitamin C 8%; Calcium 18%; Iron 8% • **Exchanges:** 1 Starch, 2 Lean Meat, 1 Fat • **Carbohydrate Choices:** 1

High Altitude (3500 to 6500 feet): No changes.

Blue Cheese–Club Sandwich Pie

Prep: **20 min**   Bake: **25 min**   Stand: **5 min**

6 servings

8 slices bacon, crisply cooked and crumbled (1/2 cup)

1/2 cup finely chopped cooked chicken or turkey

1/4 cup crumbled blue cheese

1/2 cup Original Bisquick mix

1 cup milk

1/8 teaspoon pepper

2 eggs

1 medium tomato, cut into wedges

3/4 cup shredded lettuce

1 Heat oven to 400°. Spray pie plate, 9 × 1 1/4 inches, with cooking spray. Sprinkle bacon, chicken and 2 tablespoons of the cheese in pie plate.

2 Stir Bisquick mix, milk, pepper and eggs in medium bowl with wire whisk or fork until blended. Pour into pie plate.

3 Bake about 25 minutes or until top is golden brown and knife inserted in center comes out clean. Let stand 5 minutes before serving. Garnish with tomato, lettuce and remaining 2 tablespoons blue cheese.

Reduced-Fat Impossibly Easy Blue Cheese–Club Sandwich Pie: Use Reduced Fat Bisquick mix and fat-free (skim) milk. Substitute 3 egg whites or 1/2 cup fat-free cholesterol-free egg product for the eggs.

Impossibly Easy Cheddar Cheese–Club Sandwich Pie: Use 1/4 cup shredded Cheddar cheese instead of the 2 tablespoons blue cheese in the pie; use 1/4 cup shredded Cheddar cheese instead of the 2 tablespoons blue cheese garnish.

1 SERVING: Calories 180 (Calories from Fat 100); Fat 11g (Saturated 4g); Cholesterol 95mg; Sodium 410mg; Carbohydrate 9g (Dietary Fiber 0g); Protein 11g • **% Daily Value:** Vitamin A 8%; Vitamin C 4%; Calcium 10%; Iron 4% • **Exchanges:** 1/2 Starch, 1 1/2 High-Fat Meat • **Carbohydrate Choices:** 1/2

High Altitude (3500 to 6500 feet): No changes.

Impossibly Easy
Chicken–Asparagus Alfredo Pie

Prep: **5 min** Bake: **32 min**

6 servings

1 cup diced cooked chicken (about 5 ounces)

1 package (9 ounces) frozen asparagus cuts, thawed and drained

1 container (10 ounces) refrigerated Alfredo pasta sauce

1/2 cup Original Bisquick mix

1/2 cup milk

2 eggs

1 Heat oven to 400°. Spray pie plate, 9 × 1 1/4 inches, with cooking spray. Place chicken and asparagus in pie plate.

2 Stir 1/2 cup of the Alfredo pasta sauce, the Bisquick mix, milk and eggs in medium bowl with wire whisk or fork until blended. Pour into pie plate.

3 Bake 25 to 32 minutes or until knife inserted in center comes out clean and top is golden brown.

4 Meanwhile, heat remaining Alfredo sauce as directed on container. Spoon about 1 tablespoon sauce over each serving.

1 SERVING: Calories 300 (Calories from Fat 190); Fat 21g (Saturated 12g); Cholesterol 140mg; Sodium 410mg; Carbohydrate 12g (Dietary Fiber 1g); Protein 15g • **% Daily Value:** Vitamin A 20%; Vitamin C 8%; Calcium 18%; Iron 6% • **Exchanges:** 1 Starch, 2 Medium-Fat Meat, 2 Fat • **Carbohydrate Choices:** 1

High Altitude (3500 to 6500 feet): No changes.

Impossibly Easy
Nacho Chicken Pie

Prep: **10 min** Bake: **30 min** Stand: **5 min**
6 servings

1 package (6 ounces) refrigerated diced cooked chicken breast or 1 1/3 cups cut-up cooked chicken

1/2 cup mild salsa-flavored or jalapeño-flavored process cheese sauce

1/2 cup Original Bisquick mix

3/4 cup milk

2 eggs

Shredded lettuce, if desired

Chopped tomato, if desired

1 Heat oven to 400°. Spray pie plate, 9 × 1 1/4 inches, with cooking spray. Stir chicken and cheese sauce in pie plate; arrange evenly.

2 Stir Bisquick mix, milk and eggs in medium bowl with wire whisk or fork until blended. Pour into pie plate, lifting ingredients to allow Bisquick mixture to flow into pie plate.

3 Bake 25 to 30 minutes or until knife inserted in center comes out clean. Let stand 5 minutes before serving. Top with lettuce and tomato.

1 SERVING: Calories 180 (Calories from Fat 70); Fat 8g (Saturated 3g); Cholesterol 105mg; Sodium 320mg; Carbohydrate 9g (Dietary Fiber 0g); Protein 15g • % **Daily Value:** Vitamin A 6%; Vitamin C 0%; Calcium 12%; Iron 4% • **Exchanges:** 1/2 Starch, 2 Lean Meat, 1/2 Fat • **Carbohydrate Choices:** 1/2

High Altitude (3500 to 6500 feet): Use 3/4 cup Bisquick mix. Bake 27 to 32 minutes.

Impossibly Easy

Teriyaki Chicken Pie

Prep: **15 min** Bake: **35 min**

6 servings

1 teaspoon vegetable oil

1 package (1 pound) fresh teriyaki-flavored boneless, skinless chicken breast halves (3 or 4), cut into bite-size strips

1 can (8 ounces) sliced water chestnuts, drained

2 medium green onions, sliced (2 tablespoons)

1/2 cup shredded carrots (about 1 medium)

1/2 cup Original Bisquick mix

1 cup milk

2 eggs

1/4 cup chow mein noodles

1/4 cup teriyaki baste and glaze (from 12-ounce bottle)

1 Heat oven to 400°. Spray pie plate, 9 × 1 1/4 inches, with cooking spray.

2 Heat oil in 10-inch nonstick skillet over medium-high heat until hot. Cook chicken in oil about 5 minutes, stirring occasionally, until no longer pink in center and outside begins to brown; remove from heat. Stir in water chestnuts, onions and carrots. Spoon into pie plate.

3 Stir Bisquick mix, milk and eggs in medium bowl with wire whisk or fork until blended. Pour into pie plate.

4 Bake 25 to 35 minutes, covering with aluminum foil for last 5 minutes of baking, until knife inserted in center comes out clean. Sprinkle noodles over pie before serving. Drizzle 2 teaspoons of the teriyaki glaze over each serving.

1 SERVING: Calories 245 (Calories from Fat 70); Fat 8g (Saturated 2g); Cholesterol 120mg; Sodium 1390mg; Carbohydrate 20g (Dietary Fiber 1g); Protein 23g • **% Daily Value:** Vitamin A 38%; Vitamin C 2%; Calcium 10%; Iron 10% • **Exchanges:** 1 Starch, 1 Vegetable, 2 1/2 Lean Meat • **Carbohydrate Choices:** 1

High Altitude (3500 to 6500 feet): Use 2/3 cup Bisquick mix. Bake 35 to 45 minutes, covering with aluminum foil for last 10 minutes of baking.

Impossibly Easy
Cheesy Almond, Chicken 'n Chives Pie

Prep: **15 min**   Bake: **30 min**

6 servings

1 teaspoon butter or margarine

1 pound boneless, skinless chicken thighs, cut into bite-size pieces

1/2 teaspoon salt

1/4 teaspoon pepper

1 package (3 ounces) cream cheese, cut into 1/4-inch cubes

2 tablespoons chopped fresh chives or green onions

1/2 cup Original Bisquick mix

1 cup milk

2 eggs

2 tablespoons sliced almonds

1 Heat oven to 400°. Spray pie plate, 9 × 1 1/4 inches, with cooking spray.

2 Melt butter in 10-inch skillet over medium-high heat. Cook chicken in butter about 5 minutes, stirring frequently, until no longer pink in center and outside begins to brown. Sprinkle with salt and pepper. Place in pie plate. Top with cream cheese and chives.

3 Stir Bisquick mix, milk and eggs in medium bowl with wire whisk or fork until blended. Pour into pie plate. Sprinkle almonds over top.

4 Bake 22 to 30 minutes or until knife inserted in center comes out clean.

1 SERVING: Calories 275 (Calories from Fat 155); Fat 17g (Saturated 7g); Cholesterol 140mg; Sodium 470mg; Carbohydrate 9g (Dietary Fiber 0g); Protein 22g • % Daily Value: Vitamin A 8%; Vitamin C 0%; Calcium 10%; Iron 12% • **Exchanges:** 1/2 Starch, 3 Medium-Fat Meat • **Carbohydrate Choices:** 1/2

High Altitude (3500 to 6500 feet): Bake 27 to 32 minutes.

Impossibly Easy

Chicken and Broccoli Pie

(See photo insert)

Prep: **20 min** Bake: **40 min** Stand: **5 min**

6 servings

1 package (9 ounces) frozen broccoli cuts, thawed and drained

1 1/2 cups shredded Cheddar cheese (6 ounces)

1 cup cut-up cooked chicken or 2 cans (5 ounces each) chunk chicken, well drained

1 medium onion, chopped (1/2 cup)

1/2 cup Original Bisquick mix

1 cup milk

1/2 teaspoon salt

1/4 teaspoon pepper

2 eggs

1 Heat oven to 400°. Spray pie plate, 9 × 1 1/4 inches, with cooking spray. Sprinkle broccoli, 1 cup of the cheese, the chicken and onion in pie plate.

2 Stir remaining ingredients in medium bowl with wire whisk or fork until blended. Pour into pie plate.

3 Bake 35 to 38 minutes or until knife inserted in center comes out clean. Sprinkle with remaining 1/2 cup cheese. Bake 1 to 2 minutes longer or until cheese is melted. Let stand 5 minutes before serving.

Savory-Topped Impossibly Easy Chicken and Broccoli Pie: Mix 1/2 cup Original Bisquick mix, 1/4 cup chopped almonds or walnuts, 1/4 cup grated Parmesan cheese and 1/8 teaspoon garlic powder in small bowl. Cut in 2 tablespoons firm butter or margarine, using pastry blender or crisscrossing 2 knives, until crumbly. Sprinkle over pie before baking.

1 SERVING: Calories 260 (Calories from Fat 135); Fat 15g (Saturated 8g); Cholesterol 125mg; Sodium 580mg; Carbohydrate 12g (Dietary Fiber 2g); Protein 19g • **% Daily Value:** Vitamin A 22%; Vitamin C 14%; Calcium 24%; Iron 6% • **Exchanges:** 1 Starch, 2 1/2 Lean Meat, 1 Fat • **Carbohydrate Choices:** 1

High Altitude (3500 to 6500 feet): Bake 35 to 40 minutes.

Impossibly Easy
Turkey Ranch Pie

(See photo insert)

Prep: **10 min** Bake: **38 min** Stand: **5 min**

6 servings

1 1/2 cups cut-up
cooked turkey
or chicken

1 1/2 cups frozen
mixed vegetables
(from 1-pound bag)

1/2 cup shredded
Monterey Jack
cheese (2 ounces)

1/2 cup Original
Bisquick mix

1 envelope (1 ounce)
ranch dressing and
seasoning mix (milk
recipe)

1 cup milk

2 eggs

1 Heat oven to 400°. Spray pie plate, 9 × 1 1/4 inches, with cooking spray. Spread turkey and vegetables in pie plate. Sprinkle with cheese.

2 Stir remaining ingredients in medium bowl with wire whisk or fork until blended. Pour into pie plate.

3 Bake 33 to 38 minutes or until knife inserted in center comes out clean. Let stand 5 minutes before serving.

Reduced-Fat Impossibly Easy Turkey Ranch Pie: Use shredded reduced-fat Monterey Jack cheese, Reduced Fat Bisquick mix and fat-free (skim) milk. Substitute 3 egg whites or 1/2 cup fat-free cholesterol-free egg product for the eggs.

1 **SERVING:** Calories 195 (Calories from Fat 80); Fat 9g (Saturated 4g); Cholesterol 110mg; Sodium 610mg; Carbohydrate 12g (Dietary Fiber 1g); Protein 17g • % **Daily Value:** Vitamin A 18%; Vitamin C 6%; Calcium 18%; Iron 6% • **Diet Exchanges:** 1 Starch, 2 Lean Meat • **Carbohydrate Choices:** 1

High Altitude (3500 to 6500 feet): Bake 35 to 40 minutes.

Impossibly Easy
Turkey Club Pie

(See photo insert)

Prep: **15 min** Bake: **35 min** Stand: **5 min**

6 servings

1 1/2 cups cut-up cooked turkey or chicken

8 slices bacon, crisply cooked and crumbled (1/2 cup)

1 cup shredded Cheddar cheese (4 ounces)

1/2 cup Original Bisquick mix

1 cup milk

2 eggs

1 Heat oven to 400°. Spray pie plate, 9 × 1 1/4 inches, with cooking spray. Spread turkey, bacon and cheese in pie plate.

2 Stir remaining ingredients in medium bowl with wire whisk or fork until blended. Pour into pie plate.

3 Bake 30 to 35 minutes or until knife inserted in center comes out clean. Let stand 5 minutes before serving.

1 SERVING: Calories 270 (Calories from Fat 155); Fat 17g (Saturated 8g); Cholesterol 130mg; Sodium 460mg; Carbohydrate 8g (Dietary Fiber 0g); Protein 21g • **% Daily Value:** Vitamin A 8%; Vitamin C 0%; Calcium 18%; Iron 6% • **Exchanges:** 1/2 Starch, 3 Medium-Fat Meat • **Carbohydrate Choices:** 1/2

High Altitude (3500 to 6500 feet): No changes.

Impossibly Easy

Turkey and Mushroom Pie

Prep: **15 min** Bake: **30 min** Stand: **5 min**

6 servings

1 1/2 cups cut-up cooked turkey or chicken

1 can (4 ounces) mushroom pieces and stems, drained

4 medium green onions, sliced (1/4 cup)

1/2 teaspoon salt

1 cup shredded Swiss cheese (4 ounces)

1/2 cup Original Bisquick mix

1 cup milk

2 eggs

1 Heat oven to 400°. Spray pie plate, 9 × 1 1/4 inches, with cooking spray. Spread turkey, mushrooms and onions in pie plate. Sprinkle with salt and cheese.

2 Stir remaining ingredients in medium bowl with wire whisk or fork until blended. Pour into pie plate.

3 Bake about 30 minutes or until knife inserted in center comes out clean. Let stand 5 minutes before serving.

Reduced-Fat Impossibly Easy Turkey and Mushroom Pie: Use shredded reduced-fat Swiss cheese, Reduced Fat Bisquick mix and fat-free (skim) milk. Substitute 3 egg whites or 1/2 cup fat-free cholesterol-free egg product for the eggs.

Impossibly Easy Ham and Mushroom Pie: Use 1 1/2 cups chopped cooked ham instead of the turkey.

1 SERVING: Calories 230 (Calories from Fat 110); Fat 12g (Saturated 5g); Cholesterol 120mg; Sodium 540mg; Carbohydrate 11g (Dietary Fiber 1g); Protein 20g • % Daily Value: Vitamin A 8%; Vitamin C 2%; Calcium 26%; Iron 6% • Exchanges: 1 Starch, 2 1/2 Lean Meat, 1/2 Fat • Carbohydrate Choices: 1

High Altitude (3500 to 6500 feet): Use 2/3 cup Bisquick mix. Bake about 35 minutes.

Impossibly Easy

Savory Turkey Pie

Prep: 10 min Bake: **33 min** Stand: **5 min**

6 servings

1 1/2 cups cut-up cooked turkey or chicken

1 medium stalk celery, chopped (1/2 cup)

1 medium onion, finely chopped (1/2 cup)

1 teaspoon parsley flakes

1/2 teaspoon dried thyme leaves

1/4 teaspoon dried sage leaves

1/2 teaspoon salt

1/8 teaspoon pepper

2/3 cup Original Bisquick mix

3/4 cup milk

2 eggs

1 Heat oven to 400°. Spray pie plate, 9 × 1 1/4 inches, with cooking spray. Mix turkey, celery, onion, parsley, thyme, sage, salt and pepper in pie plate.

2 Stir remaining ingredients in medium bowl with wire whisk or fork until blended. Pour into pie plate.

3 Bake 25 to 33 minutes or until knife inserted in center comes out clean and edge is golden brown. Let stand 5 minutes before serving.

1 SERVING: Calories 170 (Calories from Fat 65); Fat 7g (Saturated 2g); Cholesterol 100mg; Sodium 460mg; Carbohydrate 12g (Dietary Fiber 1g); Protein 14g • % Daily Value: Vitamin A 4%; Vitamin C 0%; Calcium 8%; Iron 6% • **Exchanges:** 1 Starch, 1 1/2 Lean Meat • **Carbohydrate Choices:** 1

High Altitude (3500 to 6500 feet): Bake 30 to 35 minutes.

Seafood Pie
page 92

Apricot Pie
page 124

Sausage
Breakfast Pie
page 64

Cheeseburger
Pie
page 14

Taco Pie
page 17

Chicken
and
Broccoli Pie
page 46

French
Apple Pie
page 122

Turkey
Club Pie
page 48

FAVORITE Impossibly Easy

Turkey and Stuffing Pie

Prep: **15 min** Bake: **35 min** Stand: **5 min**

6 servings

2 cups cut-up cooked turkey or chicken

1/2 teaspoon seasoned salt

1 cup leftover cooked bread stuffing

4 medium green onions, thinly sliced (1/4 cup)

1/2 cup cooked green peas

1/2 cup Original Bisquick mix

1 cup milk

2 eggs

Turkey gravy, heated, if desired

1 Heat oven to 400°. Spray pie plate, 9 × 1 1/4 inches, with cooking spray. Spread turkey in pie plate; sprinkle with seasoned salt. Separate stuffing into small pieces; arrange on turkey. Top with onions and peas.

2 Stir Bisquick mix, milk and eggs in medium bowl with wire whisk or fork until blended. Pour into pie plate.

3 Bake 30 to 35 minutes or until knife inserted in center comes out clean. Let stand 5 minutes before serving. Serve with gravy.

1 SERVING: Calories 240 (Calories from Fat 90); Fat 10g (Saturated 3g); Cholesterol 115mg; Sodium 530mg; Carbohydrate 18g (Dietary Fiber 1g); Protein 19g • **% Daily Value:** Vitamin A 8%; Vitamin C 2%; Calcium 10%; Iron 10% • **Exchanges:** 1 Starch, 2 1/2 Lean Meat, 1/2 Fat • **Carbohydrate Choices:** 1

High Altitude (3500 to 6500 feet): No changes.

Impossibly Easy
Turkey Tetrazzini Pie

Prep: **15 min**   Bake: **36 min**   Stand: **5 min**

6 servings

1/2 cup 2-inch pieces uncooked spaghetti

1 cup diced cooked turkey

1/2 cup frozen early June peas (from 1-pound bag)

1 jar (2 ounces) diced pimientos, drained

1 jar (4 1/2 ounces) sliced mushrooms, drained

1/8 teaspoon pepper

1/4 cup grated Parmesan cheese

1/2 cup Original Bisquick mix

1 cup milk

2 eggs

1 Heat oven to 400°. Spray pie plate, 9 × 1 1/4 inches, with cooking spray. Cook and drain spaghetti as directed on package.

2 Stir together spaghetti, turkey, peas, pimientos, mushrooms, pepper and cheese in large bowl. Spread in pie plate.

3 Stir remaining ingredients in same large bowl with wire whisk or fork until blended. Pour into pie plate.

4 Bake 28 to 36 minutes or until knife inserted in center is set. Let stand 5 minutes before serving.

1 **SERVING:** Calories 180 (Calories from Fat 65); Fat 7g (Saturated 3g); Cholesterol 95mg; Sodium 380mg; Carbohydrate 15g (Dietary Fiber 2g); Protein 14g • % **Daily Value:** Vitamin A 10%; Vitamin C 8%; Calcium 14%; Iron 8% • **Exchanges:** 1 Starch, 2 Lean Meat • **Carbohydrate Choices:** 1

High Altitude (3500 to 6500 feet): Bake 30 to 38 minutes.

Turkey Taco Pie

Prep: 15 min   Bake: 35 min   Stand: 5 min

6 servings

1 pound ground
turkey breast

1 medium onion,
chopped (1/2 cup)

1 envelope
(1 1/4 ounces)
taco seasoning mix

1 can (4 1/2 ounces)
chopped green
chiles, undrained

1/2 cup Original
Bisquick mix

1 cup milk

2 eggs

1 medium tomato,
chopped (3/4 cup)

1/2 cup shredded
Monterey Jack
cheese (2 ounces)

1 Heat oven to 400°. Spray pie plate, 9 × 1 1/4 inches, with cooking spray. Cook turkey and onion in 10-inch skillet over medium-high heat 8 to 10 minutes, stirring occasionally, until turkey is no longer pink; drain. Stir in taco seasoning mix. Spread in pie plate. Sprinkle with chiles.

2 Stir Bisquick mix, milk and eggs in medium bowl with wire whisk or fork until blended. Pour into pie plate.

3 Bake 25 minutes. Top with tomato and cheese. Bake 8 to 10 minutes longer or until cheese is melted. Let stand 5 minutes before serving.

Crowd-Size Impossibly Easy Turkey Taco Pie: Double all ingredients. Spray 13 × 9 × 2-inch baking dish with cooking spray. Cook turkey and onion in 12-inch skillet 10 to 12 minutes, until turkey is no longer pink. Stir Bisquick mixture in large bowl. Bake 30 minutes. Top with tomato and cheese; bake 8 to 10 minutes longer.

Impossibly Easy Beef Taco Pie: Use lean ground beef instead of ground turkey breast.

1 SERVING: Calories 260 (Calories from Fat 100); Fat 11g (Saturated 4g); Cholesterol 130mg; Sodium 610mg; Carbohydrate 16g (Dietary Fiber 2g); Protein 24g • % Daily Value: Vitamin A 22%; Vitamin C 12%; Calcium 18%; Iron 10% • Exchanges: 1 Starch, 3 Lean Meat, 1/2 Fat • Carbohydrate Choices: 1

High Altitude (3500 to 6500 feet): No changes.

3

Ham,
Sausage
and
Bacon
Pies

= Favorite

Impossibly Easy
Ham, Apple and Cheddar Pie

(See photo insert)

Prep: **10 min**   Bake: **40 min**   Stand: **5 min**

6 servings

1 1/2 cups cut-up fully cooked ham

1 cup shredded Cheddar cheese (4 ounces)

4 medium green onions, sliced (1/4 cup)

1 small cooking apple, peeled and chopped (1/2 cup)

1/2 cup Original Bisquick mix

1 cup milk

1/8 teaspoon pepper

2 eggs

1 Heat oven to 400°. Spray pie plate, 9 × 1 1/4 inches, with cooking spray. Sprinkle ham, cheese, onions and apple in pie plate.

2 Stir remaining ingredients in medium bowl with wire whisk or fork until blended. Pour over ham mixture.

3 Bake 35 to 40 minutes or until knife inserted in center comes out clean. Let stand 5 minutes before serving.

Impossibly Easy Bacon, Apple and Cheese Pie: Substitute 12 slices bacon, crisply cooked and crumbled (3/4 cup), for the ham, and shredded Swiss or Colby-Monterey Jack cheese for the Cheddar.

1 SERVING: Calories 230 (Calories from Fat 115); Fat 13g (Saturated 6g); Cholesterol 115mg; Sodium 800mg; Carbohydrate 12g (Dietary Fiber 1g); Protein 17g • Vitamin A 8%; Vitamin C 2%; Calcium 18%; Iron 6% • **Exchanges:** 1 Starch, 2 Lean Meat, 1 Fat • **Carbohydrate Choices:** 1

High Altitude (3500 to 6500 feet): Bake about 45 minutes.

Ham and Swiss Pie

Prep: **10 min** Bake: **40 min** Stand: **5 min**

6 servings

1 1/2 cups cut-up fully cooked ham

1 cup shredded Swiss cheese (4 ounces)

4 medium green onions, sliced (1/4 cup)

1/2 cup Original Bisquick mix

1 cup milk

1/4 teaspoon salt

1/8 teaspoon pepper

2 eggs

1 medium tomato, sliced, if desired

1 medium green bell pepper, cut into rings, if desired

1 Heat oven to 400°. Spray pie plate, 9 × 1 1/4 inches, with cooking spray. Sprinkle ham, cheese and onions in pie plate.

2 Stir remaining ingredients except tomato and bell pepper in medium bowl with wire whisk or fork until blended. Pour into pie plate.

3 Bake 35 to 40 minutes or until knife inserted in center comes out clean. Let stand 5 minutes before serving. Garnish with tomato and bell pepper.

1 SERVING: Calories 230 (Calories from Fat 110); Fat 12g (Saturated 6g); Cholesterol 110mg; Sodium 830mg; Carbohydrate 12g (Dietary Fiber 0g); Protein 18g • **% Daily Value:** Vitamin A 12%; Vitamin C 20%; Calcium 26%; Iron 6% • **Exchanges:** 1/2 Starch, 1 Vegetable, 2 Lean Meat, 1 Fat • **Carbohydrate Choices:** 1

High Altitude (3500 to 6500 feet): No changes.

Impossibly Easy
Three–Cheese and Ham Pie

Prep: **10 min** Bake: **30 min** Stand: **5 min**

6 servings

1 cup cut-up fully cooked ham

1/2 cup small curd creamed cottage cheese

1/2 cup shredded mozzarella cheese (2 ounces)

1/2 cup shredded Cheddar cheese (2 ounces)

1/4 cup chopped onion

1/2 cup Original Bisquick mix

1 cup milk

2 eggs

1 Heat oven to 400°. Spray pie plate, 9 × 1 1/4 inches, with cooking spray. Mix ham, cheeses and onion in small bowl. Spread in pie plate.

2 Stir remaining ingredients in medium bowl with wire whisk or fork until blended. Pour into pie plate.

3 Bake about 30 minutes or until knife inserted in center comes out clean. Let stand 5 minutes before serving.

1 SERVING: Calories 215 (Calories from Fat 110); Fat 12g (Saturated 6g); Cholesterol 105mg; Sodium 700mg; Carbohydrate 10g (Dietary Fiber 0g); Protein 16g • % **Daily Value:** Vitamin A 8%; Vitamin C 0%; Calcium 20%; Iron 4% • **Exchanges:** 1/2 Starch, 2 Medium-Fat Meat, 1/2 Fat • **Carbohydrate Choices:** 1/2

High Altitude (3500 to 6500 feet): Bake 35 to 40 minutes.

Impossibly Easy

Ham, Cheese and Green Bean Pie

Prep: **15 min** Bake: **40 min** Stand: **5 min**

6 servings

2 1/4 cups frozen cut green beans (from 1-pound bag), thawed and drained

1 cup cubed fully cooked ham

1/2 cup Original Bisquick mix

1/2 cup small curd creamed cottage cheese

1/2 cup sour cream

2 tablespoons butter or margarine, melted

2 eggs

1 medium tomato, thinly sliced

1/4 cup grated Parmesan cheese

1 Heat oven to 350°. Spray pie plate, 9 × 1 1/4 inches, with cooking spray. Sprinkle beans and ham in pie plate.

2 Stir remaining ingredients except tomato and Parmesan cheese in medium bowl with wire whisk or fork until blended. Pour into pie plate. Arrange tomato slices on top. Sprinkle with Parmesan cheese.

3 Bake 35 to 40 minutes or until knife inserted in center comes out clean. Let stand 5 minutes before serving.

Reduced-Fat Impossibly Easy Ham, Cheese and Green Bean Pie: Use Reduced Fat Bisquick mix, reduced-fat small curd creamed cottage cheese and reduced-fat sour cream. Substitute 3 egg whites or 1/2 cup fat-free cholesterol-free egg product for the eggs.

Impossibly Easy Ham, Cheese and Asparagus Pie: Substitute 1 package (9 ounces) frozen asparagus cuts, rinsed with cold water to thaw and drained, for the green beans.

1 SERVING: Calories 230 (Calories from Fat 135); Fat 15g (Saturated 8g); Cholesterol 110mg; Sodium 680mg; Carbohydrate 11g (Dietary Fiber 2g); Protein 13g • % Daily Value: Vitamin A 16%; Vitamin C 4%; Calcium 12%; Iron 6% • **Exchanges:** 1/2 Starch, 1/2 Vegetable, 1 1/2 Medium-Fat Meat, 1 1/2 Fat • **Carbohydrate Choices:** 1

High Altitude (3500 to 6500 feet): Heat oven to 375°. Use 2/3 cup Bisquick mix. Bake 38 to 43 minutes.

Impossibly Easy

Cheesy Ham
and Broccoli Pie

Prep: **10 min**   Bake: **35 min**   Stand: **5 min**

6 servings

2 cups frozen broccoli cuts (from 1-pound bag), thawed and drained

1 cup cubed fully cooked ham

1/4 cup chopped onion

1 cup shredded Cheddar cheese (4 ounces)

1/2 cup Original Bisquick mix

1 cup small curd creamed cottage cheese

1/4 cup milk

1/4 teaspoon ground red pepper (cayenne)

2 eggs

1 Heat oven to 400°. Spray pie plate, 9 × 1 1/4 inches, with cooking spray. Sprinkle broccoli, ham, onion and 1/2 cup of the Cheddar cheese in pie plate.

2 Stir remaining ingredients in medium bowl with wire whisk or fork until blended. Pour into pie plate.

3 Bake about 30 minutes or until knife inserted in center comes out clean. Sprinkle with remaining 1/2 cup Cheddar cheese. Bake about 5 minutes longer or until cheese is melted. Let stand 5 minutes before serving.

Reduced-Fat Impossibly Easy Cheesy Ham and Broccoli Pie: Use shredded reduced-fat Cheddar cheese, Reduced Fat Bisquick mix, reduced-fat small curd creamed cottage cheese and fat-free (skim) milk. Substitute 3 egg whites or 1/2 cup fat-free cholesterol-free egg product for the eggs.

1 SERVING: Calories 240 (Calories from Fat 115); Fat 13g (Saturated 7g); Cholesterol 110mg; Sodium 780mg; Carbohydrate 12g (Dietary Fiber 2g); Protein 19g • **% Daily Value:** Vitamin A 28%; Vitamin C 20%; Calcium 18%; Iron 8% • **Exchanges:** 1/2 Starch, 1 Vegetable, 2 1/2 Lean Meat, 1 Fat • **Carbohydrate Choices:** 1

High Altitude (3500 to 6500 feet): Bake about 33 minutes. After adding cheese, bake about 3 minutes longer.

Impossibly Easy
Ham, Swiss and Asparagus Pie

Prep: **15 min** Bake: **40 min** Stand: **5 min**

6 servings

1 cup chopped fully cooked ham

1 cup shredded Swiss cheese (4 ounces)

1/2 pound fresh asparagus, cut into 1-inch pieces (1 cup)*

2 medium green onions, sliced (2 tablespoons)

1/2 cup Original Bisquick mix

1 cup milk

1/8 teaspoon pepper

2 eggs

1 Heat oven to 400°. Spray pie plate, 9 × 1 1/4 inches, with cooking spray. Sprinkle ham, 1/2 cup of the cheese, the asparagus and onions in pie plate.

2 Stir remaining ingredients in medium bowl with wire whisk or fork until blended. Pour into pie plate, lifting ingredients to allow baking mix mixture to flow into pie plate.

3 Bake 35 to 40 minutes or until knife inserted in center comes out clean. Sprinkle with remaining 1/2 cup cheese. Let stand 5 minutes before serving.

1 package (9 ounces) frozen asparagus cuts, rinsed with cold water to thaw and drained, can be used instead of the fresh asparagus.

Reduced-Fat Impossibly Easy Ham, Swiss and Asparagus Pie: Use shredded reduced-fat Swiss cheese, Reduced Fat Bisquick mix and fat-free (skim) milk. Substitute 3 egg whites or 1/2 cup fat-free cholesterol-free egg product for the eggs.

1 SERVING: Calories 240 (Calories from Fat 115); Fat 13g (Saturated 7g); Cholesterol 110mg; Sodium 780mg; Carbohydrate 12g (Dietary Fiber 2g); Protein 19g • **% Daily Value:** Vitamin A 28%; Vitamin C 20%; Calcium 18%; Iron 8% • **Exchanges:** 1/2 Starch, 1 Vegetable, 2 1/2 Lean Meat, 1 Fat • **Carbohydrate Choices:** 1

High Altitude (3500 to 6500 feet): Bake 40 to 45 minutes.

Impossibly Easy
Ham, Mushroom and Green Bean Pie

Prep: **15 min** Bake: **40 min** Stand: **5 min**

6 servings

1 cup cubed fully cooked ham

2 1/4 cups frozen cut green beans (from 1-pound bag), thawed and drained

1 jar (4 1/2 ounces) sliced mushrooms, drained

1 cup shredded Swiss cheese (4 ounces)

1/2 cup Original Bisquick mix

1 cup milk

2 eggs

1 Heat oven to 400°. Spray pie plate, 9 × 1 1/4 inches, with cooking spray. Sprinkle ham, beans, mushrooms and cheese in pie plate.

2 Stir remaining ingredients in medium bowl with wire whisk or fork until blended. Pour into pie plate.

3 Bake 35 to 40 minutes or until knife inserted in center comes out clean. Let stand 5 minutes before serving.

Reduced-Fat Impossibly Easy Ham, Mushroom and Green Bean Pie: Use shredded reduced-fat Swiss cheese, Reduced Fat Bisquick mix and fat-free (skim) milk. Substitute 3 egg whites or 1/2 cup fat-free cholesterol-free egg product for the eggs.

1 SERVING: Calories 210 (Calories from Fat 100); Fat 11g (Saturated 5g); Cholesterol 150mg; Sodium 660mg; Carbohydrate 12g (Dietary Fiber 2g); Protein 16g • % **Daily Value:** Vitamin A 12%; Vitamin C 0%; Calcium 28%; Iron 8% • **Exchanges:** 1/2 Starch, 1/2 Vegetable, 2 Medium-Fat Meat • **Carbohydrate Choices:** 1

High Altitude (3500 to 6500 feet): Heat oven to 425°. Bake 37 to 42 minutes.

Impossibly Easy
Ham Salad Pie

Prep: **15 min** Bake: **35 min** Stand: **5 min**

6 servings

1/2 cup frozen green peas (from 1-pound bag), rinsed with cold water to thaw and drained

1 cup cubed fully cooked ham

1/2 cup shredded Cheddar cheese (2 ounces)

1/4 cup chopped green onions or chopped onion

1/2 cup Original Bisquick mix

1 cup milk

1/4 cup mayonnaise or salad dressing

1 tablespoon yellow mustard

1/4 teaspoon pepper

2 eggs

1 Heat oven to 400°. Spray pie plate, 9 × 1 1/4 inches, with cooking spray. Sprinkle peas, ham, cheese and onions in pie plate.

2 Stir remaining ingredients in medium bowl with wire whisk or fork until blended. Pour into pie plate.

3 Bake 30 to 35 minutes or until knife inserted in center comes out clean. Let stand 5 minutes before serving.

Reduced-Fat Impossibly Easy Ham Salad Pie: Use shredded reduced-fat Cheddar cheese, Reduced Fat Bisquick, fat-free (skim) milk and reduced-fat mayonnaise or salad dressing. Substitute 3 egg whites or 1/2 cup fat-free cholesterol-free egg product for the eggs.

1 SERVING: Calories 235 (Calories from Fat 145); Fat 16g (Saturated 5g); Cholesterol 100mg; Sodium 670mg; Carbohydrate 11g (Dietary Fiber 1g); Protein 12g • **% Daily Value:** Vitamin A 8%; Vitamin C 2%; Calcium 14%; Iron 6% • **Exchanges:** 1 Starch, 1 1/2 Medium-Fat Meat, 1 Fat • **Carbohydrate Choices:** 1

High Altitude (3500 to 6500 feet): No changes.

Impossibly Easy

Sausage Breakfast Pie

Prep: **20 min**   Bake: **37 min**   Stand: **5 min**

6 servings

(See photo insert)

1 package (12 ounces)
bulk pork sausage

1 small bell pepper,
chopped (1/2 cup)

1 medium onion,
chopped (1/2 cup)

1 1/2 cups frozen
hash brown potatoes

1 cup shredded
Cheddar cheese
(4 ounces)

1/2 cup Original
Bisquick mix

1 cup milk

1/8 teaspoon pepper

2 eggs

1 Heat oven to 400°. Spray pie plate, 9 × 1 1/4 inches, with cooking spray. Cook sausage, bell pepper and onion in 10-inch skillet over medium heat 8 to 10 minutes, stirring occasionally, until sausage is no longer pink; drain. Mix sausage mixture, potatoes and 1/2 cup of the cheese. Spread in pie plate.

2 Stir remaining ingredients in medium bowl with wire whisk or fork until blended. Pour into pie plate.

3 Bake 30 to 35 minutes or until knife inserted in center comes out clean. Sprinkle with remaining 1/2 cup cheese. Bake 1 to 2 minutes longer or just until cheese is melted. Let stand 5 minutes before serving.

Crowd-Size Impossibly Easy Sausage Breakfast Pie: Double all ingredients. Spray 13 × 9 × 2-inch baking dish with cooking spray. Cook sausage mixture in 12-inch skillet. Stir Bisquick mixture in large bowl. Bake 35 to 40 minutes.

1 SERVING: Calories 315 (Calories from Fat 170); Fat 19g (Saturated 8g); Cholesterol 115mg; Sodium 790mg; Carbohydrate 21g (Dietary Fiber 2g); Protein 15g • **% Daily Value:** Vitamin A 8%; Vitamin C 14%; Calcium 18%; Iron 6% • **Exchanges:** 1 1/2 Starch, 1 1/2 Medium-Fat Meat, 2 Fat • **Carbohydrate Choices:** 1 1/2

High Altitude (3500 to 6500 feet): No changes.

Sausage and Apple Pie

Prep: **10 min**   Bake: **45 min**

6 servings

1/2 pound bulk
pork sausage

1 cup shredded
Cheddar cheese
(4 ounces)

2 medium apples,
thinly sliced (2 cups)

3/4 cup Original
Bisquick mix

3/4 cup milk

4 eggs

1/4 teaspoon
ground cinnamon

1 Heat oven to 325°. Spray pie plate,
9 × 1 1/4 inches, with cooking spray.
Cook sausage in 10-inch skillet over
medium heat 6 to 8 minutes, stirring
occasionally, until no longer pink; drain.
Mix sausage, cheese and apples. Spread
in pie plate.

2 Stir Bisquick mix, milk and eggs in
medium bowl with wire whisk or fork
until blended. Pour into pie plate.
Sprinkle with cinnamon.

3 Bake about 45 minutes or until knife
inserted in center comes out clean.

1 **SERVING:** Calories 290 (Calories from Fat 160); Fat 18g (Saturated 8g); Cholesterol 180mg;
Sodium 620mg; Carbohydrate 18g (Dietary Fiber 1g); Protein 14g • % **Daily Value:** Vitamin A 10%;
Vitamin C 2%; Calcium 18%; Iron 6% • **Exchanges:** 1/2 Starch, 1/2 Fruit, 2 High-Fat Meat, 1/2 Fat •
Carbohydrate Choices: 1

High Altitude (3500 to 6500 feet): Heat oven to 350°. Bake 50 to 55 minutes.

Impossibly Easy
Italian Sausage Pie

Prep: **10 min** Bake: **30 min** Stand: **5 min**

6 servings

1/2 pound bulk
Italian sausage

1 cup shredded
mozzarella cheese
(4 ounces)

1/2 cup Original
Bisquick mix

1 cup milk

2 eggs

1 Heat oven to 400°. Spray pie plate, 9 × 1 1/4 inches, with cooking spray. Cook sausage in 10-inch skillet over medium heat 6 to 8 minutes, stirring occasionally, until no longer pink; drain. Sprinkle sausage and cheese in pie plate.

2 Stir remaining ingredients in medium bowl with wire whisk or fork until blended. Pour into pie plate.

3 Bake about 30 minutes or until knife inserted in center comes out clean. Let stand 5 minutes before serving.

Reduced-Fat Impossibly Easy Italian Sausage Pie: Use shredded part-skim mozzarella cheese, Reduced Fat Bisquick mix and fat-free (skim) milk. Substitute 3 egg whites or 1/2 cup fat-free cholesterol-free egg product for the eggs.

1 **SERVING:** Calories 225 (Calories from Fat 125); Fat 14g (Saturated 6g); Cholesterol 105mg; Sodium 540mg; Carbohydrate 9g (Dietary Fiber 0g); Protein 15g • **% Daily Value:** Vitamin A 6%; Vitamin C 0%; Calcium 22%; Iron 4% • **Exchanges:** 1/2 Starch, 2 Medium-Fat Meat, 1 Fat • **Carbohydrate Choices:** 1/2

High Altitude (3500 to 6500 feet): No changes.

Impossibly Easy

Italian Sausage and Mixed-Veggie Pie

Prep: **15 min** Bake: **35 min** Stand: **5 min**

6 servings

1/2 pound bulk Italian sausage

2 cups frozen mixed vegetables (from 1-pound bag), thawed and well drained

1/2 cup Original Bisquick mix

1 cup milk

1/2 teaspoon salt

1/4 teaspoon pepper

2 eggs

1 Heat oven to 400°. Spray pie plate, 9 × 1 1/4 inches, with cooking spray. Cook sausage in 10-inch skillet over medium heat 6 to 8 minutes, stirring occasionally, until no longer pink; drain. Spread sausage in pie plate. Sprinkle with vegetables.

2 Stir remaining ingredients in medium bowl with wire whisk or fork until blended. Pour into pie plate.

3 Bake 30 to 35 minutes or until knife inserted in center comes out clean. Let stand 5 minutes before serving.

Reduced-Fat Impossibly Easy Italian Sausage and Mixed-Veggie Pie: Use Reduced Fat Bisquick mix and fat-free (skim) milk. Substitute 3 egg whites or 1/2 cup fat-free cholesterol-free egg product for the eggs.

1 SERVING: Calories 190 (Calories from Fat 100); Fat 11g (Saturated 4g); Cholesterol 95mg; Sodium 650mg; Carbohydrate 11g (Dietary Fiber 1g); Protein 11g • % Daily Value: Vitamin A 28%; Vitamin C 12%; Calcium 10%; Iron 6% • Exchanges: 1/2 Starch, 1/2 Vegetable, 1 1/2 Medium-Fat Meat, 1/2 Fat • Carbohydrate Choices: 1

High Altitude (3500 to 6500 feet): Bake 33 to 38 minutes.

Impossibly Easy
Spicy Pork and Chicken Pie

Prep: **20 min** Bake: **37 min** Stand: **5 min**

6 servings

1/2 pound bulk pork sausage

1 cup chopped cooked chicken or turkey

1 package (9 ounces) frozen spinach, thawed and squeezed to drain

4 medium green onions, sliced (1/4 cup)

1 cup shredded Cheddar cheese (4 ounces)

1/2 cup Original Bisquick mix

1 cup milk

1/2 teaspoon ground red pepper (cayenne)

1/4 teaspoon ground sage

2 eggs

1 Heat oven to 400°. Spray pie plate, 9 × 1 1/4 inches, with cooking spray. Cook sausage in 10-inch skillet over medium heat 6 to 8 minutes, stirring occasionally, until no longer pink; drain. Sprinkle sausage, chicken, spinach, onions and 1/2 cup of the cheese in pie plate.

2 Stir remaining ingredients in medium bowl with wire whisk or fork until blended. Pour into pie plate.

3 Bake 30 to 35 minutes or until knife inserted in center comes out clean. Sprinkle with remaining 1/2 cup cheese. Bake about 2 minutes longer or until cheese is melted. Let stand 5 minutes before serving.

Reduced-Fat Impossibly Easy Spicy Pork and Chicken Pie: Used shredded reduced-fat Cheddar cheese, Reduced Fat Bisquick mix and fat-free (skim) milk. Substitute 3 egg whites or 1/2 cup fat-free cholesterol-free egg product for the eggs.

1 **SERVING:** Calories 275 (Calories from Fat 155); Fat 17g (Saturated 8g); Cholesterol 130mg; Sodium 580mg; Carbohydrate 11g (Dietary Fiber 1g); Protein 20g • % Daily Value: Vitamin A 58%; Vitamin C 4%; Calcium 22%; Iron 10% • **Exchanges:** 1/2 Starch, 1 Vegetable, 2 1/2 Medium-Fat Meat, 1/2 Fat • **Carbohydrate Choices: 1**

High Altitude (3500 to 6500 feet): No changes.

Impossibly Easy

Sausage–Spinach Pie

Prep: **15 min**   Bake: **33 min**   Stand: **5 min**

6 servings

1 pound bulk pork sausage

1 medium onion, chopped (1/2 cup)

1 1/2 cups frozen cut leaf spinach (from 1-pound bag), thawed and squeezed to drain

1/2 teaspoon salt

1/4 teaspoon pepper

1/2 cup Original Bisquick mix

1 cup milk

2 eggs

3/4 cup shredded Cheddar cheese (3 ounces)

1 Heat oven to 400°. Spray pie plate, 9 × 1 1/4 inches, with cooking spray. Cook sausage and onion in 10-inch skillet over medium heat 8 to 10 minutes, stirring occasionally, until sausage is no longer pink; drain. Mix sausage and onion, spinach, salt and pepper in skillet. Spread in pie plate.

2 Stir Bisquick mix, milk and eggs in medium bowl with wire whisk or fork until blended. Pour into pie plate.

3 Bake 25 minutes. Sprinkle with cheese. Bake 5 to 8 minutes longer or until knife inserted in center comes out clean. Let stand 5 minutes before serving.

1 SERVING: Calories 300 (Calories from Fat 190); Fat 21g (Saturated 9g); Cholesterol 125mg; Sodium 970mg; Carbohydrate 11g (Dietary Fiber 1g); Protein 17g • % **Daily Value:** Vitamin A 34%; Vitamin C 2%; Calcium 20%; Iron 8% • **Exchanges:** 1/2 Starch, 1/2 Vegetable, 2 Medium-Fat Meat, 2 Fat • **Carbohydrate Choices:** 1

High Altitude (3500 to 6500 feet): No changes.

Impossibly Easy
Sausage and Cheese Pie

Prep: **15 min** Bake: **25 min**

6 servings

1 package (12 ounces) pork sausage links

1 medium onion, chopped (1/2 cup)

1/3 cup chopped green bell pepper

1 cup shredded Cheddar cheese (4 ounces)

1/2 cup Original Bisquick mix

1 cup evaporated milk (from 12-ounce can)

2 eggs

1 Heat oven to 400°. Spray pie plate, 9 × 1 1/4 inches, with cooking spray. Cook sausage links as directed on package; drain. Arrange sausage links 1/2 to 1 inch apart in pie plate. Sprinkle onion, bell pepper and cheese over sausage.

2 Stir remaining ingredients in medium bowl with wire whisk or fork until blended. Pour into pie plate.

3 Bake about 25 minutes or until knife inserted in center comes out clean.

1 SERVING: Calories 450 (Calories from Fat 315); Fat 35g (Saturated 15g); Cholesterol 150mg; Sodium 1070mg; Carbohydrate 13g (Dietary Fiber 1g); Protein 21g • **% Daily Value:** Vitamin A 10%; Vitamin C 6%; Calcium 26%; Iron 8% • **Exchanges:** 1 Starch, 3 Medium-Fat Meat, 3 Fat • **Carbohydrate Choices:** 1

High Altitude (3500 to 6500 feet): No changes.

Impossibly Easy
Oktoberfest Pie

Prep: **10 min** Bake: **35 min** Stand: **5 min**

6 servings

1/2 pound fully cooked bratwurst (about 3), cut into 3/4-inch pieces

1 can (8 ounces) sauerkraut, drained (1 1/3 cups)

1 cup shredded Swiss cheese (4 ounces)

3/4 cup Original Bisquick mix

1/2 cup milk

1/2 cup regular or nonalcoholic beer

2 eggs

1 Heat oven to 400°. Spray pie plate, 9 × 1 1/4 inches, with cooking spray. Sprinkle bratwurst, sauerkraut and cheese in pie plate.

2 Stir remaining ingredients in medium bowl with wire whisk or fork until blended. Pour into pie plate.

3 Bake 30 to 35 minutes or until knife inserted in center comes out clean. Let stand 5 minutes before serving.

1 SERVING: Calories 290 (Calories from Fat 180); Fat 20g (Saturated 8g); Cholesterol 110mg; Sodium 930mg; Carbohydrate 14g (Dietary Fiber 1g); Protein 14g • % Daily Value: Vitamin A 6%; Vitamin C 4%; Calcium 24%; Iron 8% • **Exchanges:** 1 Starch, 1 1/2 High-Fat Meat, 1 1/2 Fat • **Carbohydrate Choices:** 1

High Altitude (3500 to 6500 feet): No changes.

Impossibly Easy
Pizza Pie

Prep: **10 min** Bake: **35 min** Stand: **5 min**

6 servings

1 medium onion,
chopped (1/2 cup)

1/3 cup grated
Parmesan cheese

1/2 cup Original
Bisquick mix

1 cup milk

2 eggs

1 can (8 ounces)
pizza sauce

1/2 package
(3-ounce size)
sliced pepperoni

1/4 cup chopped
green bell pepper

3/4 cup shredded
mozzarella cheese
(3 ounces)

1 Heat oven to 400°. Spray pie plate,
9 × 1 1/4 inches, with cooking spray.
Sprinkle onion and Parmesan cheese
in pie plate.

2 Stir Bisquick, milk and eggs in medium
bowl with wire whisk or fork until
blended. Pour into pie plate.

3 Bake 20 minutes. Spread with pizza
sauce; top with remaining ingredients.
Bake 10 to 15 minutes longer or until
cheese is light brown. Let stand 5 minutes before serving. Sprinkle with additional Parmesan cheese if desired.

Crowd-Size Impossibly Easy Pizza Pie: Double
all ingredients. Spray 13 × 9 × 2-inch baking
dish with cooking spray. Bake 25 minutes.
Spread with pizza sauce; top with remaining
ingredients. Bake 10 to 15 minutes longer.

1 SERVING: Calories 225 (Calories from Fat 115); Fat 13g (Saturated 6g); Cholesterol 95mg;
Sodium 690mg; Carbohydrate 14g (Dietary Fiber 1g); Protein 13g • % **Daily Value:** Vitamin A 10%;
Vitamin C 12%; Calcium 26%; Iron 6% • **Exchanges:** 1 Starch, 1 1/2 Medium-Fat Meat, 1 Fat •
Carbohydrate Choices: 1

High Altitude (3500 to 6500 feet): Increase first bake time to 30 minutes.

Impossibly Easy
Chicago–Style
Pizza

Prep: **15 min**   Bake: **35 min**   Stand: **5 min**

6 servings

1 pound bulk Italian sausage

1 can (14 1/2 ounces) diced tomatoes with garlic, basil and oregano, drained

2 cups shredded mozzarella cheese (8 ounces)

1/2 cup Original Bisquick mix

1 cup milk

2 eggs

1 Heat oven to 400°. Spray pie plate, 9 × 1 1/4 inches, with cooking spray. Cook sausage in 10-inch skillet over medium heat 8 to 10 minutes, stirring occasionally, until no longer pink; drain. Spread tomatoes in pie plate. Sprinkle with 1 cup of the cheese. Top with sausage and remaining 1 cup cheese.

2 Stir remaining ingredients in medium bowl with wire whisk or fork until blended. Pour into pie plate.

3 Bake 30 to 35 minutes or until knife inserted in center comes out clean. Let stand 5 minutes before serving.

Crowd-Size Impossibly Easy Chicago-Style Pizza: Double all ingredients. Spray 13 × 9 × 2-inch baking dish with cooking spray. Cook sausage in 12-inch skillet. Stir Bisquick mixture in large bowl. Bake 30 to 35 minutes.

1 SERVING: Calories 380 (Calories from Fat 225); Fat 25g (Saturated 11g); Cholesterol 135mg; Sodium 990mg; Carbohydrate 13g (Dietary Fiber 1g); Protein 26g • **% Daily Value:** Vitamin A 12%; Vitamin C 8%; Calcium 38%; Iron 10% • **Exchanges:** 1/2 Starch, 1 Vegetable, 3 Medium-Fat Meat, 2 Fat • **Carbohydrate Choices:** 1

High Altitude (3500 to 6500 feet): Use 10 × 1 1/2-inch pie plate.

Impossibly Easy
Bacon and Swiss Pie

Prep: **20 min** Bake: **40 min** Stand: **5 min**

6 servings

12 slices bacon, crisply cooked and crumbled (3/4 cup)

1 cup shredded Swiss cheese (4 ounces)

1/3 cup chopped onion

1/2 cup Original Bisquick mix

1 cup milk

1/8 teaspoon pepper

2 eggs

1 Heat oven to 400°. Spray pie plate, 9 × 1 1/4 inches, with cooking spray. Sprinkle bacon, cheese and onion in pie plate.

2 Stir remaining ingredients in medium bowl with wire whisk or fork until blended. Pour into pie plate.

3 Bake 35 to 40 minutes or until knife inserted in center comes out clean. Let stand 5 minutes before serving.

1 SERVING: Calories 225 (Calories from Fat 135); Fat 15g (Saturated 7g); Cholesterol 100mg; Sodium 430mg; Carbohydrate 10g (Dietary Fiber 0g); Protein 13g • **% Daily Value:** Vitamin A 6%; Vitamin C 0%; Calcium 24%; Iron 4% • **Exchanges:** 1/2 Starch, 2 Medium-Fat Meat, 1 Fat • **Carbohydrate Choices:** 1/2

High Altitude (3500 to 6500 feet): Bake 28 to 33 minutes.

Impossibly Easy
BLT Pie

Prep: **10 min** Bake: **30 min** Stand: **5 min**

6 servings

12 slices bacon, crisply cooked and crumbled (3/4 cup)

1 cup shredded Swiss cheese (4 ounces)

1/2 cup Original Bisquick mix

1/3 cup mayonnaise or salad dressing

3/4 cup milk

1/8 teaspoon pepper

2 eggs

2 tablespoons mayonnaise or salad dressing

1 cup shredded lettuce

6 thin slices tomato

1 Heat oven to 400°. Spray pie plate, 9 × 1 1/4 inches, with cooking spray. Layer bacon and cheese in pie plate.

2 Stir Bisquick mix, 1/3 cup mayonnaise, the milk, pepper and eggs in medium bowl with wire whisk or fork until blended. Pour into pie plate.

3 Bake 25 to 30 minutes or until top is golden brown and knife inserted in center comes out clean. Let stand 5 minutes before serving. Spread 2 tablespoons mayonnaise over top of pie. Sprinkle with lettuce. Place tomato slices on lettuce.

1 **SERVING:** Calories 345 (Calories from Fat 250); Fat 28g (Saturated 9g); Cholesterol 110mg; Sodium 530mg; Carbohydrate 10g (Dietary Fiber 0g); Protein 13g • % **Daily Value:** Vitamin A 8%; Vitamin C 2%; Calcium 24%; Iron 4% • **Exchanges:** 1/2 Starch, 2 High-Fat Meat, 2 Fat • **Carbohydrate Choices:** 1/2

High Altitude (3500 to 6500 feet): Bake 30 to 35 minutes.

Calico Corn and Bacon Pie

Prep: **20 min** Bake: **30 min** Stand: **5 min**

6 servings

8 slices bacon, crisply cooked and crumbled (1/2 cup)

1 small onion, chopped (1/4 cup)

1/4 cup chopped green bell pepper

1 can (7 ounces) vacuum-packed whole kernel corn, drained

1 jar (2 ounces) diced pimientos, drained

2/3 cup Original Bisquick mix

1 cup milk

1/8 teaspoon pepper

2 eggs

Sour cream, if desired

1 Heat oven to 400°. Spray pie plate, 9 × 1 1/4 inches, with cooking spray. Reserve 2 tablespoons of the bacon. Sprinkle remaining bacon, the onion, bell pepper, corn and pimientos in pie plate.

2 Stir remaining ingredients except sour cream in medium bowl with wire whisk or fork until blended. Pour into pie plate.

3 Bake about 30 minutes or until knife inserted in center comes out clean. Let stand 5 minutes before serving. Garnish with sour cream and reserved bacon.

1 SERVING: Calories 190 (Calories from Fat 90); Fat 10g (Saturated 4g); Cholesterol 85mg; Sodium 440mg; Carbohydrate 18g (Dietary Fiber 1g); Protein 8g • % **Daily Value:** Vitamin A 8%; Vitamin C 14%; Calcium 8%; Iron 6% • **Exchanges:** 1 Starch, 1/2 High-Fat Meat, 1 Vegetable, 1 Fat • **Carbohydrate Choices:** 1

High Altitude (3500 to 6500 feet): No changes.

Impossibly Easy

Bacon, Roasted Peppers and Feta Pie

Prep: **25 min**   Bake: **35 min**   Stand: **5 min**

6 servings

12 slices bacon, crisply cooked and crumbled (3/4 cup)

4 medium green onions, sliced (1/4 cup)

1/3 cup chopped roasted red bell peppers (from 7-ounce jar), drained

1/2 cup crumbled feta cheese

3/4 cup Original Bisquick mix

1 cup milk

1 teaspoon dried basil leaves

3 eggs

1 Heat oven to 400°. Spray pie plate, 9 × 1 1/4 inches, with cooking spray. Mix bacon, onions and bell peppers in pie plate. Sprinkle with cheese.

2 Stir remaining ingredients in medium bowl with wire whisk or fork until blended. Pour into pie plate.

3 Bake 30 to 35 minutes or until knife inserted in center comes out clean. Let stand 5 minutes before serving.

Reduced-Fat Impossibly Easy Bacon, Roasted Peppers and Feta Pie: Use Reduced Fat Bisquick mix and fat-free (skim) milk. Substitute 5 egg whites or 3/4 cup fat-free cholesterol-free egg product for the eggs.

1 SERVING: 220 Calories (Calories from Fat 125); Fat 14g (Saturated 6g); Cholesterol 130mg; Sodium 610mg; Carbohydrate 13g (Dietary Fiber 0g); Protein 11g • **% Daily Value:** Vitamin A 18%; Vitamin C 16%; Calcium 16%; Iron 6% • **Exchanges:** 1 Starch, 1 High-Fat Meat, 1 Fat • **Carbohydrate Choices:** 1

High Altitude (3500 to 6500 feet): No changes.

Impossibly Easy

Bacon, Onion and Herb Pie

Prep: **15 min** Bake: **35 min**

6 servings

1/4 cup butter
or margarine

3 medium onions,
thinly sliced and
separated into rings

12 slices bacon,
crisply cooked and
crumbled (3/4 cup)

1 cup Original
Bisquick mix

1 1/4 cups milk

2 teaspoons
Worcestershire
sauce

3 eggs

1/4 teaspoon dried
savory leaves

1/4 teaspoon dried
basil leaves

1/4 teaspoon
parsley flakes

1 Heat oven to 400°. Spray pie plate, 9 × 1 1/4 inches, with cooking spray. Melt butter in 10-inch skillet over medium-high heat. Cook onions in butter 3 to 4 minutes, stirring frequently, until softened. Arrange half of the onions evenly in pie plate; sprinkle with half of the bacon. Top with remaining onions and bacon.

2 Stir Bisquick mix, milk, Worcestershire sauce and eggs in medium bowl with wire whisk or fork until blended. Pour into pie plate. Mix herbs in small bowl; crush slightly. Sprinkle evenly over pie.

3 Bake about 35 minutes until knife inserted in center comes out clean.

1 SERVING: Calories 305 (Calories from Fat 180); Fat 20g (Saturated 9g); Cholesterol 140mg; Sodium 610mg; Carbohydrate 20g (Dietary Fiber 1g); Protein 11g • % Daily Value: Vitamin A 12%; Vitamin C 2%; Calcium 12%; Iron 8% • Exchanges: 1 Starch, 1 High-Fat Meat, 2 1/2 Fat • Carbohydrate Choices: 1

High Altitude (3500 to 6500 feet): No changes.

Impossibly Easy
Hot Dog 'n Cheese Pie

Prep: **15 min**   Bake: **30 min**   Stand: **5 min**

6 servings

1/2 pound hot dogs, cut into 1/4-inch pieces

1/4 cup chopped onion, if desired

1/2 cup Original Bisquick mix

1 cup milk

2 eggs

1 cup shredded Cheddar cheese (4 ounces)

Ketchup and mustard, if desired

1 Heat oven to 400°. Spray pie plate, 9 × 1 1/4 inches, with cooking spray. Layer hot dog pieces and onion in pie plate.

2 Stir Bisquick mix, milk and eggs in medium bowl with wire whisk or fork until blended. Pour into pie plate. Sprinkle with cheese.

3 Bake 25 to 30 minutes or until knife inserted in center comes out clean. Let stand 5 minutes before serving. Serve with ketchup and mustard.

Reduced-Fat Impossibly Easy Hot Dog 'n Cheese Pie: Use reduced-fat hot dogs, Reduced Fat Bisquick mix, fat-free (skim) milk and shredded reduced-fat Cheddar cheese. Substitute 3 egg whites or 1/2 cup fat-free cholesterol-free egg product for the eggs.

1 SERVING: Calories 280 (Calories from Fat 190); Fat 21g (Saturated 9g); Cholesterol 115mg; Sodium 750mg; Carbohydrate 10g (Dietary Fiber 0g); Protein 13g • **% Daily Value:** Vitamin A 8%; Vitamin C 0%; Calcium 18%; Iron 4% • **Exchanges:** 1/2 Starch, 1 1/2 High-Fat Meat, 2 Fat • **Carbohydrate Choices:** 1/2

High Altitude (3500 to 6500 feet): Use 2/3 cup Bisquick mix.

4

Fish and Seafood Favorites

⭐ = Favorite

Impossibly Easy
Tuna Pie

Prep: **15 min** Bake: **30 min** Stand: **5 min**

6 servings

1 can (6 ounces) tuna in water, drained

1/4 cup thinly sliced celery

2 cups shredded Cheddar cheese (8 ounces)

4 medium green onions, sliced (1/4 cup)

1/2 cup Original Bisquick mix

1 cup milk

1/2 teaspoon lemon juice

1/4 teaspoon salt

1/8 teaspoon pepper

2 eggs

1 Heat oven to 400°. Spray pie plate, 9 × 1 1/4 inches, with cooking spray. Sprinkle tuna, celery, cheese and onions in pie plate.

2 Stir remaining ingredients in medium bowl with wire whisk or fork until blended. Pour into pie plate.

3 Bake about 30 minutes or until knife inserted in center comes out clean. Let stand 5 minutes before serving.

Reduced-Fat Impossibly Easy Tuna Pie: Use shredded reduced-fat Cheddar cheese, Reduced Fat Bisquick mix and fat-free (skim) milk. Substitute 3 egg whites or 1/2 cup fat-free cholesterol-free egg product for the eggs.

1 SERVING: Calories 275 (Calories from Fat 155); Fat 17g (Saturated 9g); Cholesterol 120mg; Sodium 520mg; Carbohydrate 10g (Dietary Fiber 0g); Protein 21g • **% Daily Value:** Vitamin A 12%; Vitamin C 2%; Calcium 28%; Iron 8% • **Exchanges:** 1/2 Starch, 3 Medium-Fat Meat • **Carbohydrate Choices:** 1/2

High Altitude (3500 to 6500 feet): Use 2/3 cup Bisquick mix. Bake about 35 minutes.

Impossibly Easy
Cheesy Tuna Pie

Prep: **15 min** Bake: **35 min** Stand: **5 min**

6 servings

1 cup shredded American and Cheddar Jack cheese blend (4 ounces)

1/3 cup frozen green peas (from 1-pound bag), thawed and drained

4 medium green onions, sliced (1/4 cup)

1 can (6 ounces) tuna, well drained

1 jar (2 ounces) diced pimientos, drained

1 package (3 ounces) cream cheese, cut into 1/4-inch cubes

3/4 cup Original Bisquick mix

1 cup milk

1/8 teaspoon ground nutmeg

3 eggs

1 Heat oven to 400°. Spray pie plate, 9 × 1 1/4 inches, with cooking spray. Mix cheese blend, peas, onions, tuna and pimientos in pie plate. Top with cream cheese cubes.

2 Stir remaining ingredients in medium bowl with wire whisk or fork until blended. Pour into pie plate.

3 Bake 30 to 35 minutes or until knife inserted in center comes out clean (some cheese may adhere to knife). Let stand 5 minutes before serving.

Crowd-Size Impossibly Easy Cheesy Tuna Pie: Double all ingredients. Spray 13 × 9 × 2-inch baking dish with cooking spray. Stir Bisquick mixture in large bowl. Bake 38 to 43 minutes.

1 SERVING: Calories 275 (Calories from Fat 155); Fat 17g (Saturated 9g); Cholesterol 150mg; Sodium 490mg; Carbohydrate 14g (Dietary Fiber 1g); Protein 17g • % Daily Value: Vitamin A 20%; Vitamin C 8%; Calcium 22%; Iron 10% • **Exchanges:** 1 Starch, 2 Medium-Fat Meat, 1 Fat • Carbohydrate Choices: 1

High Altitude (3500 to 6500 feet): Bake 35 to 40 minutes.

Impossibly Easy
Tuna, Tomato and Cheddar Pie

Prep: **20 min** Bake: **35 min** Stand: **5 min**

6 servings

1 tablespoon butter or margarine

1 large onion, chopped (1 cup)

1 can (6 ounces) tuna, drained

1 cup shredded Cheddar cheese (4 ounces)

1/2 cup Original Bisquick mix

1 cup milk

1/8 teaspoon pepper

2 eggs

1 medium tomato, thinly sliced

1 Heat oven to 400°. Spray pie plate, 9 × 1 1/4 inches, with cooking spray. Melt butter in 10-inch skillet over low heat. Cook onion in butter, stirring occasionally, until tender. Sprinkle tuna, 1/2 cup of the cheese and the onion in pie plate.

2 Stir remaining ingredients except tomato in medium bowl with wire whisk or fork until blended. Pour into pie plate.

3 Bake 25 to 30 minutes or until knife inserted in center comes out clean. Top with tomato slices and remaining 1/2 cup cheese. Bake 3 to 5 minutes longer or until cheese is melted. Let stand 5 minutes before serving.

Impossibly Easy Tuna Melt Pie: Use 2 tablespoons butter or margarine instead of 1 tablespoon, and substitute 1 cup cubed process cheese spread loaf (4 ounces) for the shredded Cheddar cheese.

1 SERVING: Calories 225 (Calories from Fat 110); Fat 12g (Saturated 7g); Cholesterol 110mg; Sodium 410mg; Carbohydrate 12g (Dietary Fiber 1g); Protein 17g • % Daily Value: Vitamin A 12%; Vitamin C 4%; Calcium 18%; Iron 6% • **Exchanges:** 1 Starch, 2 Medium-Fat Meat • **Carbohydrate Choices:** 1

High Altitude (3500 to 6500 feet): No changes.

Impossibly Easy

Italian Tuna Pie

Prep: **25 min**   Bake: **30 min**   Stand: **5 min**

6 servings

1 can (6 ounces) tuna, drained

1 medium onion, chopped (1/2 cup)

1/2 cup chopped green bell pepper

1 medium tomato, chopped (3/4 cup)

1 can (2 1/4 ounces) sliced ripe olives, drained

1/2 cup Original Bisquick mix

1 cup milk

1 teaspoon dried oregano leaves

1/2 teaspoon salt

1/2 teaspoon dried basil leaves

1/4 teaspoon pepper

2 eggs

1 clove garlic, finely chopped

1 Heat oven to 400°. Spray pie plate, 9 × 1 1/4 inches, with cooking spray. Layer tuna, onion, bell pepper, tomato and olives in pie plate.

2 Stir remaining ingredients in medium bowl with wire whisk or fork until blended. Pour into pie plate.

3 Bake 25 to 30 minutes or until knife inserted in center comes out clean. Let stand 5 minutes before serving.

Reduced-Fat Impossibly Easy Italian Tuna Pie: Use Reduced Fat Bisquick mix and fat-free (skim) milk. Substitute 3 egg whites or 1/2 cup fat-free cholesterol-free egg product for the eggs.

1 SERVING: Calories 150 (Calories from Fat 55); Fat 6g (Saturated 2g); Cholesterol 80mg; Sodium 580mg; Carbohydrate 12g (Dietary Fiber 1g); Protein 12g • % **Daily Value:** Vitamin A 8%; Vitamin C 14%; Calcium 10%; Iron 8% • **Exchanges:** 1/2 Starch, 1 Vegetable, 1 1/2 Lean Meat • **Carbohydrate Choices:** 1

High Altitude (3500 to 6500 feet): Bake 30 to 35 minutes.

Impossibly Easy
Tuna–Tomato Pie

Prep: **10 min** Bake: **30 min** Stand: **5 min**

6 servings

1 can (6 ounces) tuna in water, drained

1 medium tomato, chopped (3/4 cup)

1/3 cup shredded mozzarella cheese

1 tablespoon chopped fresh or 1 teaspoon dried basil leaves

1/2 cup Original Bisquick mix

1 cup milk

1/2 teaspoon salt, if desired

1/4 teaspoon pepper

2 eggs

1 Heat oven to 400°. Spray pie plate, 9 × 1 1/4 inches, with cooking spray. Sprinkle tuna, tomato, cheese and basil in pie plate.

2 Stir remaining ingredients in medium bowl with wire whisk or fork until blended. Pour into pie plate, lifting ingredients to allow Bisquick mixture to flow into pie plate.

3 Bake about 30 minutes or until knife inserted in center comes out clean. Let stand 5 minutes before serving.

Reduced-Fat Impossibly Easy Tuna-Tomato Pie: Use shredded part-skim mozzarella cheese, fat-free (skim) milk and Reduced Fat Bisquick mix. Substitute 3 egg whites or 1/2 cup fat-free cholesterol-free egg product for the eggs.

1 SERVING: Calories 135 (Calories from Fat 45); Fat 5g (Saturated 2g); Cholesterol 85mg; Sodium 310mg; Carbohydrate 9g (Dietary Fiber 0g); Protein 13g • **% Daily Value:** Vitamin A 8%; Vitamin C 2%; Calcium 12%; Iron %6 • **Exchanges:** 1/2 Starch, 2 Very Lean Meat, 1/2 Fat • **Carbohydrate Choices:** 1/2

High Altitude (3500 to 6500 feet): Use 3/4 cup Bisquick mix. Bake about 33 minutes.

Tuna and Green Bean Pie

Prep: **10 min** Bake: **35 min**

6 servings

1 can (12 ounces)
tuna, drained

1 can (14.5 ounces)
cut green beans,
drained

3/4 cup French-fried
onions (from 2.8-
ounce can)

1/2 cup Original
Bisquick mix

1/2 cup sour cream

1/2 cup milk

1/2 teaspoon lemon
pepper

2 eggs

1 Heat oven to 400°. Spray pie plate, 9 × 1 1/4 inches, with cooking spray.

2 Toss together tuna, green beans and 1/4 cup of the onions in medium bowl. Spoon into pie plate.

3 Stir remaining ingredients in same medium bowl with wire whisk or fork until blended. Pour into pie plate, lifting ingredients to allow Bisquick mixture to flow into pie plate.

4 Bake 25 minutes. Top with remaining 1/2 cup onions. Bake 5 to 10 minutes longer or until center is set and edge is golden brown.

1 **SERVING**: Calories 235 (Calories from Fat 100); Fat 11g (Saturated 4g); Cholesterol 100mg; Sodium 610mg; Carbohydrate 14g (Dietary Fiber 2g); Protein 20g • % Daily Value: Vitamin A 16%; Vitamin C 2%; Calcium 8%; Iron 12% • **Exchanges:** 1 Starch, 2 1/2 Lean Meat, 1/2 Fat • Carbohydrate Choices: 1

High Altitude (3500 to 6500 feet): No changes.

Impossibly Easy
Crabmeat Pie

Prep: **10 min** Bake: **30 min** Stand: **5 min**

6 servings

1 package (6 ounces) frozen ready-to-serve crabmeat, thawed and drained*

1 jar (4 1/2 ounces) sliced mushrooms, drained

1 cup shredded Monterey Jack cheese (4 ounces)

1/2 cup Original Bisquick mix

1/2 cup sour cream

1/2 cup small curd creamed cottage cheese

1/4 cup grated Parmesan cheese

1/8 teaspoon ground red pepper (cayenne)

2 eggs

1 Heat oven to 400°. Spray pie plate, 9 × 1 1/4 inches, with cooking spray. Layer crabmeat, mushrooms and Monterey Jack cheese in pie plate.

2 Stir remaining ingredients in medium bowl with wire whisk or fork until blended. Pour into pie plate.

3 Bake about 30 minutes or until knife inserted in center comes out clean. Let stand 5 minutes before serving.

*1 can (6 ounces) crabmeat, drained and cartilage removed, can be used instead of the frozen crabmeat.

Reduced-Fat Impossibly Easy Crabmeat Pie: Use shredded reduced-fat Monterey Jack cheese, Reduced Fat Bisquick mix, reduced-fat sour cream and reduced-fat small curd creamed cottage cheese. Substitute 3 egg whites or 1/2 cup fat-free cholesterol-free egg product for the eggs.

1 SERVING: Calories 245 (Calories from Fat 135); Fat 15g (Saturated 8g); Cholesterol 135mg; Sodium 590mg; Carbohydrate 9g (Dietary Fiber 1g); Protein 18g • **% Daily Value:** Vitamin A 10%; Vitamin C 0%; Calcium 28%; Iron 6% • **Exchanges:** 1/2 Starch, 2 1/2 Medium-Fat Meat, 1/2 Fat • **Carbohydrate Choices:** 1/2

High Altitude (3500 to 6500 feet): No changes.

Impossibly Easy
Deviled
Crabmeat Pie

Prep: **15 min** Bake: **35 min** Stand: **5 min**

6 servings

1 package (6 ounces) frozen ready-to-serve crabmeat, thawed and drained*

1/4 cup chopped onion

1/4 cup chopped celery

1/4 cup shredded carrot (about 1 small)

1/4 cup grated Parmesan cheese

1/2 cup Original Bisquick mix

1 cup milk

1 1/2 teaspoons Worcestershire sauce

1/4 teaspoon pepper

2 eggs

1 Heat oven to 350°. Spray pie plate, 9 × 1 1/4 inches, with cooking spray. Layer crabmeat, onion, celery, carrot and cheese in pie plate.

2 Stir remaining ingredients in medium bowl with wire whisk or fork until blended. Pour into pie plate.

3 Bake 30 to 35 minutes or until knife inserted in center comes out clean. Let stand 5 minutes before serving.

*1 can (6 ounces) crabmeat, drained and cartilage removed, can be used instead of the frozen crabmeat.

Reduced-Fat Impossibly Easy Deviled Crabmeat Pie: Use Reduced Fat Bisquick mix and fat-free (skim) milk. Substitute 3 egg whites or 1/2 cup fat-free cholesterol-free egg product for the eggs.

1 SERVING: Calories 140 (Calories from Fat 55); Fat 6g (Saturated 2g); Cholesterol 10.5mg; Sodium 360mg; Carbohydrate 10g (Dietary Fiber 0g); Protein 12g • % Daily Value: Vitamin A 22%; Vitamin C 2%; Calcium 16%; Iron 4% • **Exchanges:** 1/2 Starch, 2 Lean Meat • **Carbohydrate Choices:** 1/2

High Altitude (3500 to 6500 feet): No changes.

Impossibly Easy
Asian Crabmeat Pie

Prep: **10 min** Bake: **35 min** Stand: **5 min**

6 servings

1 package (6 ounces) frozen ready-to-serve crabmeat, thawed and drained*

1/2 cup chopped water chestnuts (from 8-ounce can)

1 package (6 ounces) frozen snow (Chinese) pea pods, thawed, drained and coarsely chopped

1 tablespoon soy sauce

3/4 cup Original Bisquick mix

1 1/4 cups milk

1/4 teaspoon pepper

3 eggs

1 Heat oven to 400°. Spray pie plate, 9 × 1 1/4 inches, with cooking spray. Sprinkle crabmeat, water chestnuts, pea pods and soy sauce in pie plate.

2 Stir remaining ingredients in medium bowl with wire whisk or fork until blended. Pour into pie plate.

3 Bake about 35 minutes or until knife inserted in center comes out clean. Let stand 5 minutes before serving. Serve with additional soy sauce if desired.

*1 can (6 ounces) crabmeat, drained and cartilage removed, can be used instead of the frozen crabmeat.

Reduced-Fat Impossibly Easy Asian Crabmeat Pie: Use Reduced Fat Bisquick mix and fat-free (skim) milk. Substitute 5 egg whites or 3/4 cup fat-free cholesterol-free egg product for the eggs.

Impossibly Easy Asian Chicken Pie: Use 1 can (5 ounces) chunk chicken, well drained, instead of the crabmeat.

1 **SERVING:** Calories 165 (Calories from Fat 55); Fat 6g (Saturated 2g); Cholesterol 140mg; Sodium 500mg; Carbohydrate 15g (Dietary Fiber 1g); Protein 13g • % Daily Value: Vitamin A 6%; Vitamin C 12%; Calcium 14%; Iron 8% • Exchanges: 1/2 Starch, 1 Vegetable, 2 Lean Meat • Carbohydrate Choices: 1

High Altitude (3500 to 6500 feet): Bake about 40 minutes.

Impossibly Easy

Crabmeat Creole Pie

Prep: 15 min Bake: **35 min** Stand: **5 min**

6 servings

1 package (6 ounces) frozen ready-to-serve crabmeat, thawed and drained*

2 cups frozen cut okra (from 1-pound bag), thawed and drained

1 can (14 1/2 ounces) diced tomatoes, drained

1/4 cup chopped green bell pepper

4 medium green onions, sliced (1/4 cup)

1/2 teaspoon chili powder

1/8 to 1/4 teaspoon red pepper sauce

1/2 cup Original Bisquick mix

1 cup milk

1/2 teaspoon salt

1/4 teaspoon pepper

2 eggs

1 Heat oven to 400°. Spray pie plate, 9 × 1 1/4 inches, with cooking spray. Stir together crabmeat, okra, tomatoes, bell pepper, onions, chili powder and pepper sauce in medium bowl. Spread in pie plate.

2 Stir remaining ingredients in medium bowl with wire whisk or fork until blended. Pour into pie plate, gently stirring crabmeat-vegetable mixture.

3 Bake 30 to 35 minutes or until knife inserted in center comes out clean. Let stand 5 minutes before serving.

*1 can (6 ounces) crabmeat, drained and cartilage removed, can be used instead of the frozen crabmeat.

Reduced-Fat Impossibly Easy Crabmeat Creole Pie: Use Reduced Fat Bisquick mix and fat-free (skim) milk. Substitute 3 egg whites or 1/2 cup fat-free cholesterol-free egg product for the eggs.

1 SERVING: Calories 155 (Calories from Fat 45); Fat 5g (Saturated 2g); Cholesterol 100mg; Sodium 570mg; Carbohydrate 16g (Dietary Fiber 3g); Protein 12g • **% Daily Value:** Vitamin A 14%; Vitamin C 20%; Calcium 18%; Iron 10% • **Exchanges:** 1/2 Starch, 2 Vegetable, 1 Lean Meat • **Carbohydrate Choices:** 1

High Altitude (3500 to 6500 feet): Use 1 1/2 cups okra and 3/4 cup Bisquick mix. Bake 35 to 40 minutes.

Impossibly Easy
Seafood Pie

(See photo insert)

Prep: **15 min**   Bake: **40 min**   Stand: **5 min**

6 servings

1 package (6 ounces) frozen ready-to-serve crabmeat, thawed and drained*

1 cup shredded sharp Cheddar cheese (4 ounces)

1 package (3 ounces) cream cheese, cut into 1/4-inch cubes and softened

4 medium green onions, sliced (1/4 cup)

1 jar (2 ounces) diced pimientos, drained, if desired

1/2 cup Original Bisquick mix

1 cup milk

1/2 teaspoon salt

1/8 teaspoon ground nutmeg

2 eggs

1 Heat oven to 400°. Spray pie plate, 9 × 1 1/4 inches, with cooking spray. Stir together crabmeat, cheeses, onions and pimientos in pie plate.

2 Stir remaining ingredients in medium bowl with wire whisk or fork until blended. Pour into pie plate.

3 Bake 35 to 40 minutes or until golden brown and knife inserted in center comes out clean (some cream cheese may stick to knife). Let stand 5 minutes before serving.

1 can (6 ounces) crabmeat, drained and cartilage removed, can be used instead of the frozen crabmeat.

Reduced-Fat Impossibly Easy Seafood Pie: Use shredded reduced-fat Cheddar cheese, reduced-fat cream cheese (Neufchâtel), Reduced Fat Bisquick mix and fat-free (skim) milk. Substitute 3 egg whites or 1/2 cup fat-free cholesterol-free egg product for the eggs.

Impossibly Easy Shrimp Seafood Pie: Substitute 1 package (4 ounces) frozen cooked salad shrimp, thawed and drained, or 1 can (4 to 4 1/2 ounces) shrimp, rinsed and drained, for the crabmeat.

1 SERVING: Calories 230 (Calories from Fat 135); Fat 15g (Saturated 9g); Cholesterol 135mg; Sodium 620mg; Carbohydrate 10g (Dietary Fiber 1g); Protein 15g • **% Daily Value:** Vitamin A 18%; Vitamin C 8%; Calcium 22%; Iron 8% • **Exchanges:** 1/2 Starch, 2 Lean Meat, 2 Fat • **Carbohydrate Choices:** 1/2

High Altitude (3500 to 6500 feet): No changes.

Impossibly Easy
Shrimp Pie

Prep: **10 min** Bake: **35 min** Stand: **5 min**

6 servings

1 1/4 cups frozen
cooked salad
shrimp (6 ounces),
thawed and drained

4 medium green
onions, sliced
(1/4 cup)

1/2 teaspoon dried
basil leaves

1 cup shredded
Swiss cheese
(4 ounces)

3/4 cup Original
Bisquick mix

1 1/4 cups milk

1/2 teaspoon salt

1/4 teaspoon pepper

3 eggs

1 Heat oven to 400°. Spray pie plate,
9 × 1 1/4 inches, with cooking spray.
Layer shrimp, onions, basil and cheese
in pie plate.

2 Stir remaining ingredients in medium
bowl with wire whisk or fork until
blended. Pour into pie plate.

3 Bake 30 to 35 minutes until top is
golden brown and knife inserted in
center comes out clean. Let stand
5 minutes before serving.

Reduced-Fat Impossibly Easy Shrimp Pie:
Use shredded reduced-fat Swiss cheese,
Reduced Fat Bisquick mix and fat-free (skim)
milk. Substitute 5 egg whites or 3/4 cup fat-free
cholesterol-free egg product for the eggs.

1 SERVING: Calories 220 (Calories from Fat 100); Fat 11g (Saturated 5g); Cholesterol 180mg;
Sodium 580mg; Carbohydrate 13g (Dietary Fiber 0g); Protein 17g • % **Daily Value:** Vitamin A 10%;
Vitamin C 2%; Calcium 30%; Iron 10% • **Exchanges:** 1 Starch, 2 Lean Meat, 1 Fat • **Carbohydrate Choices:** 1

High Altitude (3500 to 6500 feet): No changes.

Impossibly Easy
Shrimp and Spinach Quiche Pie

Prep: **10 min** Bake: **45 min**

6 servings

3/4 cup Original Bisquick mix

1 cup milk

1/2 teaspoon salt

1/4 teaspoon pepper

3 eggs

1 package (9 ounces) frozen creamed spinach, thawed

1 package (7 ounces) frozen cooked salad shrimp (about 1 1/2 cups), thawed, rinsed and drained

1 Heat oven to 400°. Spray pie plate, 9 × 1 1/4 inches, with cooking spray.

2 Stir Bisquick mix, milk, salt, pepper and eggs in large bowl with wire whisk or fork until blended. Gently stir in spinach and shrimp. Pour into pie plate.

3 Bake 35 to 45 minutes or until knife inserted in center comes out clean and top is golden brown.

1 SERVING: Calories 185 (Calories from Fat 70); Fat 8g (Saturated 2g); Cholesterol 175mg; Sodium 670mg; Carbohydrate 14g (Dietary Fiber 1g); Protein 14g • **% Daily Value:** Vitamin A 50%; Vitamin C 2%; Calcium 15%; Iron 12% • **Exchanges:** 1 Starch, 1 1/2 Lean Meat, 1/2 Fat • **Carbohydrate Choices:** 1

High Altitude (3500 to 6500 feet): Bake 40 to 45 minutes.

Impossibly Easy
Salmon–Dill Pie

Prep: **10 min** Bake: **35 min** Stand: **5 min**

6 servings

1 cup sour cream

1/2 teaspoon dried
dill weed

1 can (7 1/2 ounces)
salmon, drained and
flaked

1/2 teaspoon dried
dill weed

3/4 cup Original
Bisquick mix

1 1/2 cups milk

1 teaspoon lemon
juice

1/2 teaspoon salt

1/4 teaspoon pepper

3 eggs

1 Stir together sour cream and 1/2 tea-spoon dill weed in small bowl; cover and refrigerate.

2 Heat oven to 400°. Spray pie plate, 9 × 1 1/4 inches, with cooking spray. Sprinkle salmon and 1/2 teaspoon dill weed in pie plate.

3 Stir remaining ingredients in medium bowl with wire whisk or fork until blended. Pour into pie plate.

4 Bake 30 to 35 minutes or until golden brown and knife inserted in center comes out clean. Let stand 5 minutes before serving. Serve with sour cream mixture.

Reduced-Fat Impossibly Easy Salmon-Dill Pie: Use reduced-fat sour cream, Reduced Fat Bisquick mix and fat-free (skim) milk. Substitute 5 egg whites or 3/4 cup fat-free cholesterol-free egg product for the eggs.

Impossibly Easy Tuna-Dill Pie: Use 1 can (6 ounces) tuna, drained, instead of the salmon.

1 SERVING: Calories 245 (Calories from Fat 135); Fat 15g (Saturated 7g); Cholesterol 155mg; Sodium 680mg; Carbohydrate 14g (Dietary Fiber 0g); Protein 14g • **% Daily Value:** Vitamin A 10%; Vitamin C 0%; Calcium 22%; Iron 6% • **Exchanges:** 1 Starch, 1 1/2 Medium-Fat Meat, 1 Fat • **Carbohydrate Choices:** 1

High Altitude (3500 to 6500 feet): No changes.

Impossibly Easy
Salmon–Asparagus Pie

Prep: **10 min**   Bake: **37 min**   Stand: **10 min**

6 servings

(See photo insert)

1 pound fresh asparagus, cut into 1-inch pieces (2 cups)*

4 medium green onions, sliced (1/4 cup)

1 1/2 cups shredded Swiss cheese (6 ounces)

1 can (6 ounces) skinless, boneless pink salmon, drained and flaked

1/2 cup Original Bisquick mix

1 cup milk

1 1/2 teaspoons chopped fresh or 1/2 teaspoon dried basil leaves

1/8 teaspoon pepper

2 eggs

1 Heat oven to 400°. Spray pie plate, 9 × 1 1/4 inches, with cooking spray. Sprinkle asparagus, onions, 3/4 cup of the cheese and the salmon in pie plate.

2 Stir remaining ingredients in medium bowl with wire whisk or fork until blended. Pour into pie plate.

3 Bake 30 to 35 minutes or until knife inserted in center comes out clean. Sprinkle with remaining 3/4 cup cheese. Bake about 2 minutes longer or until cheese is melted. Let stand 10 minutes before serving.

*1 package (9 ounces) frozen asparagus cuts, thawed and well drained, can be used instead of the fresh asparagus. Use 3/4 cup Bisquick mix and 3/4 cup milk.

Reduced-Fat Impossibly Easy Salmon-Asparagus Pie: Use shredded reduced-fat Swiss cheese, Reduced Fat Bisquick mix and fat-free (skim) milk. Substitute 3 egg whites or 1/2 cup fat-free cholesterol-free egg product for the eggs.

1 SERVING: Calories 255 (Calories from Fat 125); Fat 14g (Saturated 7g); Cholesterol 115mg; Sodium 420mg; Carbohydrate 13g (Dietary Fiber 2g); Protein 20g • % **Daily Value:** Vitamin A 22%; Vitamin C 16%; Calcium 42%; Iron 8% • **Exchanges:** 1/2 Starch, 1 Vegetable, 2 1/2 Lean Meat, 1 Fat • **Carbohydrate Choices:** 1

High Altitude (3500 to 6500 feet): No changes.

Impossibly Easy

Firecracker Salmon Pie

Prep: **10 min** Bake: **35 min**

6 servings

2 cans (6 ounces each) skinless, boneless pink salmon, drained

1/4 cup chopped celery

1/4 cup finely chopped onion

1/2 cup Original Bisquick mix

1 cup milk

2 eggs

2 teaspoons Cajun seasoning

1/2 cup mayonnaise or salad dressing

1/2 teaspoon red pepper sauce

1 tablespoon chopped fresh parsley

1 Heat oven to 400°. Spray pie plate, 9 × 1 1/4 inches, with cooking spray.

2 Toss together salmon, celery and onion in medium bowl. Spoon into pie plate.

3 Stir Bisquick mix, milk, eggs and Cajun seasoning in same medium bowl with wire whisk or fork until blended. Pour into pie plate.

4 Bake 28 to 35 minutes or until edge is golden brown and knife inserted in center comes out clean.

5 Meanwhile, stir together mayonnaise, pepper sauce and parsley in small bowl. Top each serving with about 1 table-spoon mayonnaise mixture.

1 SERVING: Calories 305 (Calories from Fat 200); Fat 22g (Saturated 4g); Cholesterol 115mg; Sodium 610mg; Carbohydrate 10g (Dietary Fiber 1g); Protein 16g • % **Daily Value:** Vitamin A 10%; Vitamin C 2%; Calcium 20%; Iron 6% • **Exchanges:** 1/2 Starch, 2 Lean Meat, 3 1/2 Fat • **Carbohydrate Choices:** 1/2

High Altitude (3500 to 6500 feet): No changes.

5

Meatless
Pies

⭐ = Favorite

Impossibly Easy
Triple-Cheese Pie

Prep: **15 min** Bake: **35 min** Stand: **5 min**

6 servings

1/2 cup small curd creamed cottage cheese

1/2 cup shredded mozzarella cheese (2 ounces)

1/2 cup shredded Cheddar cheese (2 ounces)

1/2 cup chopped green bell pepper, if desired

1/2 cup Original Bisquick mix

1 cup milk

2 eggs

1/2 cup French-fried onions (from 2.8-ounce can)

1 Heat oven to 400°. Spray pie plate, 9 × 1 1/4 inches, with cooking spray. Stir together cheeses and bell pepper in small bowl. Spread in pie plate.

2 Stir Bisquick mix, milk and eggs in medium bowl with wire whisk or fork until blended. Pour into pie plate. Sprinkle with onions.

3 Bake about 35 minutes or until golden brown and knife inserted in center comes out clean. Let stand 5 minutes before serving.

1 SERVING: Calories 200 (Calories from Fat 110); Fat 12g (Saturated 5g); Cholesterol 90mg; Sodium 400mg; Carbohydrate 11g (Dietary Fiber 0g); Protein 12g • % Daily Value: Vitamin A 6%; Vitamin C 0%; Calcium 20%; Iron 4% • Exchanges: 1 Starch, 1 Medium-Fat Meat, 1/2 Fat • Carbohydrate Choices: 1

High Altitude (3500 to 6500 feet): Use 2/3 cup Bisquick mix. Bake about 40 minutes.

Impossibly Easy
Mac 'n Cheese
Pie

Prep: **10 min** Bake: **32 min** Stand: **5 min**

6 servings

1 cup uncooked
elbow macaroni
(3 1/2 ounces)

2 cups shredded
Cheddar cheese
(8 ounces)

1/2 cup Original
Bisquick mix

1 1/2 cups milk

1/4 teaspoon red
pepper sauce

2 eggs

1 Heat oven to 400°. Spray pie plate, 9 × 1 1/4 inches, with cooking spray. Place uncooked macaroni in pie plate. Sprinkle with 1 3/4 cups of the cheese.

2 Stir remaining ingredients in medium bowl with wire whisk or fork until blended. Pour into pie plate.

3 Cover and bake 20 minutes. Uncover and bake 5 to 10 minutes longer or until knife inserted in center comes out clean. Sprinkle with remaining 1/4 cup cheese. Bake 1 to 2 minutes longer or until cheese is melted. Let stand 5 minutes before serving.

Crowd-Size Impossibly Easy Mac 'n Cheese Pie: Double all ingredients. Spray 13 × 9 × 2-inch baking dish with cooking spray. Stir Bisquick mixture in large bowl. Cover and bake 20 minutes. Uncover and bake 10 to 15 minutes longer. Sprinkle with remaining cheese; bake 1 to 2 minutes.

1 **SERVING:** Calories 320 (Calories from Fat 155); Fat 17g (Saturated 10g); Cholesterol 115mg; Sodium 430mg; Carbohydrate 26g (Dietary Fiber 1g); Protein 17g • **% Daily Value:** Vitamin A 12%; Vitamin C 0%; Calcium 30%; Iron 8% • **Exchanges:** 2 Starch, 1 1/2 Medium-Fat Meat, 1 Fat • **Carbohydrate Choices:** 2

High Altitude (3500 to 6500 feet): Heat oven to 350°. Use 1 3/4 cups milk. Bake uncovered 40 to 45 minutes before adding 1/4 cup cheese.

Impossibly Easy
Alfredo Pie

Prep: **10 min** Bake: **25 min** Stand: **5 min**

6 servings

3/4 cup Original
Bisquick mix

1/2 cup grated
Parmesan cheese

3/4 cup whipping
(heavy) cream

1/2 cup milk

1/4 teaspoon pepper

1/8 teaspoon
ground nutmeg

2 eggs

1 Heat oven to 400°. Spray pie plate,
9 × 1 1/4 inches, with cooking spray.

2 Stir together all ingredients in medium
bowl with wire whisk or fork until
blended. Pour into pie plate.

3 Bake 20 to 25 minutes or until knife
inserted in center comes out clean.
Let stand 5 minutes before serving.

Reduced-Fat Impossibly Easy Alfredo Pie:
Use Reduced Fat Bisquick mix, grated fat-free
Parmesan cheese topping and fat-free (skim)
milk. Substitute half-and-half for the whipping
cream, and 3 egg whites or 1/2 cup fat-free
cholesterol-free egg product for the eggs.

1 SERVING: Calories 220 (Calories from Fat 145); Fat 16g (Saturated 9g); Cholesterol 110mg;
Sodium 410mg; Carbohydrate 11g (Dietary Fiber 0g); Protein 8g • % **Daily Value:** Vitamin A 10%;
Vitamin C 0%; Calcium 18%; Iron 4% • **Exchanges:** 1 Starch, 1/2 High-Fat Meat, 2 Fat • **Carbohydrate
Choices:** 1

High Altitude (3500 to 6500 feet): No changes.

Impossibly Easy

Asparagus Pie

Prep: **15 min** Bake: **35 min** Stand: **5 min**

6 servings

1 package (9 ounces)
frozen asparagus
cuts, thawed and
well drained

1 can (8 ounces)
water chestnuts,
drained and
coarsely chopped

1 jar (2 ounces)
chopped pimientos,
drained

1 medium onion,
chopped (1/2 cup)

1 cup shredded
sharp Cheddar
cheese (4 ounces)

1/2 cup Original
Bisquick mix

1 cup milk

1/2 teaspoon garlic
salt

1/4 teaspoon pepper

2 eggs

1 Heat oven to 400°. Spray pie plate,
9 × 1 1/4 inches, with cooking spray.
Layer asparagus, water chestnuts,
pimientos, onion and cheese in pie
plate.

2 Stir remaining ingredients in medium
bowl with wire whisk or fork until
blended. Pour into pie plate.

3 Bake about 35 minutes or until knife
inserted in center comes out clean.
Let stand 5 minutes before serving.
Garnish with additional chopped water
chestnuts and pimientos if desired.

Reduced-Fat Impossibly Easy Asparagus Pie:
Use shredded reduced-fat sharp Cheddar cheese,
Reduced Fat Bisquick mix and fat-free (skim)
milk. Substitute 3 egg whites or 1/2 cup fat-free
cholesterol-free egg product for the eggs.

Impossibly Easy Broccoli Pie: Substitute 1 package (9 ounces) frozen broccoli spears, thawed,
drained and cut into 1-inch pieces, for the
asparagus.

1 SERVING: Calories 200 (Calories from Fat 90); Fat 10g (Saturated 5g); Cholesterol 95mg;
Sodium 390mg; Carbohydrate 17g (Dietary Fiber 2g); Protein 11g • **% Daily Value:** Vitamin A 20%;
Vitamin C 16%; Calcium 18%; Iron 6% • **Exchanges:** 1/2 Starch, 2 Vegetable, 1 Medium-Fat Meat, 1 Fat •
Carbohydrate Choices: 1

High Altitude (3500 to 6500 feet): No changes.

Cheddar 'n Broccoli Pie

Prep: **10 min** Bake: **37 min**

6 servings

1 package (9 ounces)
frozen broccoli cuts,
thawed and drained

1 1/2 cups shredded
Cheddar cheese
(6 ounces)

1 medium onion,
chopped (1/2 cup)

1/2 cup Original
Bisquick mix

1 cup milk

1/2 teaspoon salt

1/4 teaspoon pepper

2 eggs

1 Heat oven to 400°. Spray pie plate, 9 × 1 1/4 inches, with cooking spray. Sprinkle broccoli, 1 cup of the cheese and the onion in pie plate.

2 Stir together remaining ingredients in medium bowl with wire whisk or fork until blended. Pour into pie plate.

3 Bake 30 to 35 minutes or until knife inserted in center comes out clean. Sprinkle with remaining 1/2 cup cheese. Bake 1 to 2 minutes longer or until cheese is melted.

Crowd-Size Impossibly Easy Cheddar 'n Broccoli Pie: Double all ingredients. Spray 13 × 9 × 2-inch baking dish with cooking spray. Stir Bisquick mixture in large bowl. Bake 30 to 36 minutes. Sprinkle with remaining cheese; bake 1 to 2 minutes.

1 SERVING: Calories 210 (Calories from Fat 115); Fat 13g (Saturated 7g); Cholesterol 105mg; Sodium 570mg; Carbohydrate 11g (Dietary Fiber 1g); Protein 12g • **% Daily Value:** Vitamin A 22%; Vitamin C 12%; Calcium 24%; Iron 4% • **Exchanges:** 1/2 Starch, 1 Vegetable, 1 Medium-Fat Meat, 1 1/2 Fat • **Carbohydrate Choices:** 1

High Altitude (3500 to 6500 feet): No changes.

Impossibly Easy
Broccoli–Swiss Cheese Pie

Prep: **15 min** Bake: **32 min** Stand: **5 min**

6 servings

1 package (9 ounces) frozen broccoli cuts, thawed and drained

1 1/2 cups shredded Swiss cheese (6 ounces)

2 medium green onions, sliced (2 tablespoons)

1/2 cup Original Bisquick mix

2/3 cup milk

1/4 teaspoon salt

1/8 teaspoon pepper

1/8 teaspoon ground mustard

2 eggs

1 Heat oven to 400°. Spray pie plate, 9 × 1 1/4 inches, with cooking spray. Layer broccoli, 1 cup of the cheese and the onions in pie plate.

2 Stir remaining ingredients in medium bowl with wire whisk or fork until blended. Pour into pie plate.

3 Bake 25 to 30 minutes or until knife inserted in center comes out clean. Sprinkle with remaining 1/2 cup cheese. Bake 1 to 2 minutes longer or just until cheese is melted. Let stand 5 minutes before serving.

Reduced-Fat Impossibly Easy Broccoli–Swiss Cheese Pie: Use shredded reduced-fat Swiss cheese, Reduced Fat Bisquick mix and fat-free (skim) milk. Substitute 3 egg whites or 1/2 cup fat-free cholesterol-free egg product for the eggs.

1 SERVING: Calories 205 (Calories from Fat 110); Fat 12g (Saturated 6g); Cholesterol 100mg; Sodium 360mg; Carbohydrate 11g (Dietary Fiber 1g); Protein 13g • **% Daily Value:** Vitamin A 20%; Vitamin C 12%; Calcium 34%; Iron 4% • **Exchanges:** 1/2 Starch, 1 Vegetable, 1 1/2 High-Fat Meat • **Carbohydrate Choices:** 1

High Altitude (3500 to 6500 feet): No changes.

Impossibly Easy
Broccoli Brunch Pie

Prep: **15 min**   Bake: **30 min**   Stand: **5 min**

6 servings

1 package (9 ounces) frozen broccoli cuts, thawed and drained

1 cup sour cream

1 cup small curd creamed cottage cheese

1/2 cup Original Bisquick mix

1/4 cup butter or margarine, melted

2 eggs

1 medium tomato, thinly sliced

1/4 cup grated Parmesan cheese

1 Heat oven to 350°. Spray pie plate, 9 × 1 1/4 inches, with cooking spray. Spread broccoli in pie plate.

2 Beat sour cream, cottage cheese, Bisquick mix, butter and eggs in medium bowl with wire whisk or fork until blended. Pour over broccoli. Arrange tomato slices on top. Sprinkle with Parmesan cheese.

3 Bake about 30 minutes or until golden brown and knife inserted halfway between center and edge comes out clean. Let stand 5 minutes before serving.

Crowd-Size Impossibly Easy Broccoli Brunch Pie: Double all ingredients. Spray 13 × 9 × 2-inch baking dish with cooking spray. Stir Bisquick mixture in large bowl. Bake 40 to 50 minutes.

Impossibly Easy Spinach Brunch Pie: Substitute 1 package (9 ounces) frozen spinach, cooked and drained, for the broccoli.

1 SERVING: Calories 280 (Calories from Fat 190); Fat 21g (Saturated 12g); Cholesterol 125mg; Sodium 460mg; Carbohydrate 12g (Dietary Fiber 1g); Protein 11g • **% Daily Value:** Vitamin A 30%; Vitamin C 16%; Calcium 16%; Iron 4% • **Exchanges:** 1/2 Starch, 1 Vegetable, 1 Medium-Fat Meat, 3 Fat • **Carbohydrate Choices:** 1

High Altitude (3500 to 6500 feet): Bake about 38 minutes.

Turkey
Ranch Pie
page 47

Spinach Pie
page 115

Zucchini Pie
page 117

Ham,
Apple and
Cheddar Pie
page 56

Lasagna
Pie
page 16

Broccoli
and Red
Pepper Pie
page 111

Salmon-
Asparagus Pie
page 96

Cheesecake
page 136

Mocha Fudge
Cheesecake
page 139

Grasshopper
Cheesecake
page 143

Impossibly Easy
Broccoli–Carrot Pie

Prep: **20 min** Bake: **40 min** Stand: **5 min**

6 servings

1 tablespoon butter or margarine

4 medium green onions, sliced (1/4 cup)

2 cloves garlic, finely chopped

2 1/2 cups frozen chopped broccoli (from 1-pound bag), thawed and drained

1/2 cup shredded carrots (about 1 medium)

1/2 cup small curd creamed cottage cheese

1/2 cup Original Bisquick mix

1 cup milk

1/4 teaspoon pepper

3 eggs

3 tablespoons grated Parmesan cheese

1 Heat oven to 350°. Spray pie plate, 9 × 1 1/4 inches, with cooking spray. Melt butter in 10-inch skillet over medium heat. Cook onions and garlic in butter 2 to 3 minutes, stirring occasionally, until onions are tender. Stir in broccoli and carrots. Spread broccoli mixture in pie plate. Drop cottage cheese by teaspoonfuls over broccoli mixture; spread slightly.

2 Stir Bisquick mix, milk, pepper and eggs in medium bowl with wire whisk or fork until blended. Pour into pie plate. Sprinkle with Parmesan cheese.

3 Bake 35 to 40 minutes or until edge is golden brown and center is puffed. Let stand 5 minutes before serving. Sprinkle with additional Parmesan cheese if desired.

1 SERVING: Calories 170 (Calories from Fat 80); Fat 9g (Saturated 4g); Cholesterol 120mg; Sodium 360mg; Carbohydrate 12g (Dietary Fiber 1g); Protein 10g • **% Daily Value:** Vitamin A 56%; Vitamin C 4%; Calcium 18%; Iron 6% • **Exchanges:** 1 Starch, 1 Medium-Fat Meat, 1/2 Fat • **Carbohydrate Choices:** 1

High Altitude (3500 to 6500 feet): Use 3/4 cup Bisquick mix. Bake 40 to 45 minutes.

Impossibly Easy
Cheesy Vegetable Pie

Prep: **15 min** Bake: **37 min** Stand: **5 min**

6 servings

2 1/2 cups frozen broccoli, carrots and cauliflower (from 1-pound bag), thawed, drained and large pieces cut in half

1 1/2 cups shredded Cheddar cheese (6 ounces)

1/3 cup chopped onion

1/2 cup Original Bisquick mix

1 cup milk

1/2 teaspoon salt

1/4 teaspoon pepper

2 eggs

1 Heat oven to 400°. Spray pie plate, 9 × 1 1/4 inches, with cooking spray. Stir together vegetables, 1 cup of the cheese and the onion in pie plate.

2 Stir remaining ingredients in medium bowl with wire whisk or fork until blended. Pour into pie plate.

3 Bake about 35 minutes or until knife inserted in center comes out clean. Sprinkle with remaining 1/2 cup cheese. Bake 1 to 2 minutes longer or just until cheese is melted. Let stand 5 minutes before serving.

Reduced-Fat Impossibly Easy Cheesy Vegetable Pie: Use shredded reduced-fat Cheddar cheese, Reduced Fat Bisquick mix and fat-free (skim) milk. Substitute 3 egg whites or 1/2 cup fat-free cholesterol-free egg product for the eggs.

1 SERVING: Calories 210 (Calories from Fat 115); Fat 13g (Saturated 7g); Cholesterol 105mg; Sodium 570mg; Carbohydrate 11g (Dietary Fiber 1g); Protein 12g • **% Daily Value:** Vitamin A 32%; Vitamin C 12%; Calcium 24%; Iron 4% • **Exchanges:** 1/2 Starch, 1 Vegetable, 1 High-Fat Meat, 1 Fat • **Carbohydrate Choices:** 1

High Altitude (3500 to 6500 feet): No changes.

Impossibly Easy
Veggie and Pineapple Pie

Prep: **20 min**   Bake: **40 min**   Stand: **5 min**

6 servings

1 1/2 cups frozen broccoli, carrots and cauliflower (from 1-pound bag), thawed, drained and large pieces cut in half

1 cup shredded Cheddar cheese (4 ounces)

1/4 cup chopped onion

1/4 cup raisins

1 can (8 ounces) crushed pineapple, drained

1/2 cup Original Bisquick mix

1 cup milk

1/4 teaspoon ground mustard

1/4 teaspoon dried thyme leaves

2 eggs

1 Heat oven to 400°. Spray pie plate, 9 × 1 1/4 inches, with cooking spray. Sprinkle vegetables, cheese, onion, raisins and pineapple in pie plate.

2 Stir remaining ingredients in medium bowl with wire whisk or fork until blended. Pour into pie plate.

3 Bake 35 to 40 minutes or until knife inserted in center comes out clean (some cheese may adhere to knife). Let stand 5 minutes before serving.

Reduced-Fat Impossibly Easy Veggie and Pineapple Pie: Use shredded reduced-fat Cheddar cheese, Reduced Fat Bisquick mix and fat-free (skim) milk. Substitute 3 egg whites or 1/2 cup fat-free cholesterol-free egg product for the eggs.

1 SERVING: Calories 215 (Calories from Fat 90); Fat 10g (Saturated 5g); Cholesterol 95mg; Sodium 310mg; Carbohydrate 21g (Dietary Fiber 2g); Protein 10g • **% Daily Value:** Vitamin A 22%; Vitamin C 10%; Calcium 18%; Iron 6% • **Exchanges:** 1 Starch, 1 Vegetable, 1 Medium-Fat Meat, 1 Fat • **Carbohydrate Choices:** 1 1/2

High Altitude (3500 to 6500 feet): No changes.

Impossibly Easy
Carrot and Rice Pie

Prep: **15 min** Bake: **35 min** Stand: **5 min**

6 servings

1 cup finely shredded carrots (3 to 4 medium)

3/4 cup uncooked instant rice

2/3 cup shredded Cheddar cheese

1/3 cup chopped onion

1 teaspoon dried basil leaves

3/4 cup Original Bisquick mix

1 1/2 cups milk

1/4 cup butter or margarine, softened

1/2 teaspoon salt

1/4 teaspoon pepper

3 eggs

1 Heat oven to 400°. Spray pie plate, 9 × 1 1/4 inches, with cooking spray. Stir together carrots, rice, cheese, onion and basil in medium bowl. Spread in pie plate.

2 Stir remaining ingredients in medium bowl with wire whisk or fork until blended. Pour into pie plate.

3 Bake 30 to 35 minutes until knife inserted in center comes out clean. Let stand 5 minutes before serving.

1 SERVING: Calories 315 (Calories from Fat 160); Fat 18g (Saturated 10g); Cholesterol 145mg; Sodium 610mg; Carbohydrate 27g (Dietary Fiber 1g); Protein 11g • **% Daily Value:** Vitamin A 80%; Vitamin C 2%; Calcium 18%; Iron 8% • **Exchanges:** 2 Starch, 1/2 High-Fat Meat, 2 1/2 Fat • **Carbohydrate Choices:** 2

High Altitude (3500 to 6500 feet): No changes.

Impossibly Easy

Broccoli and Red Pepper Pie

(See photo insert)

Prep: **20 min** Bake: **35 min** Stand: **5 min**

6 servings

2 cups chopped broccoli

1/3 cup chopped onion

1/3 cup chopped red or yellow bell pepper

1 cup shredded Cheddar cheese (4 ounces)

1/2 cup Original Bisquick mix

1 cup milk

1/2 teaspoon salt

1/4 teaspoon pepper

2 eggs

1 Heat oven to 400°. Spray pie plate, 9 × 1 1/4 inches, with cooking spray. Heat 1 inch water (salted if desired) to boiling in 2-quart saucepan. Add broccoli; cover and heat to boiling. Cook about 5 minutes or until almost tender; drain thoroughly.

2 Stir together broccoli, onion, bell pepper and cheese in pie plate. Stir remaining ingredients in medium bowl with wire whisk or fork until blended. Pour into pie plate.

3 Bake uncovered 30 to 35 minutes or until golden brown and knife inserted in center comes out clean. Let stand 5 minutes before serving.

Reduced-Fat Impossibly Easy Broccoli and Red Pepper Pie: Use shredded reduced-fat Cheddar cheese, Reduced Fat Bisquick mix and fat-free (skim) milk. Substitute 1/2 cup fat-free cholesterol-free egg product for the eggs.

1 SERVING: Calories 170 (Calories from Fat 90); Fat 10g (Saturated 5g); Cholesterol 95mg; Sodium 500mg; Carbohydrate 11g (Dietary Fiber 1g); Protein 10g • **% Daily Value:** Vitamin A 16%; Vitamin C 14%; Calcium 18%; Iron 4% • **Exchanges:** 1/2 Starch; 1 Medium-Fat Meat; 1 Vegetable; 1 Fat • **Carbohydrate Choices:** 1

High Altitude (3500 to 6500 feet): Heat oven to 425°. Bake about 30 minutes.

Impossibly Easy
Cheesy Chile Pie

Prep: **10 min**   Bake: **30 min**   Stand: **5 min**

6 servings

1 can (4 1/2 ounces)
chopped green
chiles, well drained

2 cups shredded
Cheddar cheese
(8 ounces)

1 teaspoon
chopped fresh
cilantro or parsley

3/4 cup Original
Bisquick mix

1 1/2 cups milk

3 eggs

Salsa, if desired

1 Heat oven to 400°. Spray pie plate,
9 × 1 1/4 inches, with cooking spray.
Sprinkle chiles, cheese and cilantro in
pie plate.

2 Stir remaining ingredients except salsa
in medium bowl with wire whisk or
fork until blended. Pour into pie plate.

3 Bake 25 to 30 minutes or until knife
inserted in center comes out clean. Let
stand 5 minutes before serving. Serve
with salsa.

**Reduced-Fat Impossibly Easy Cheesy Chile
Pie:** Use shredded reduced-fat Cheddar cheese,
Reduced Fat Bisquick mix and fat-free (skim)
milk. Substitute 5 egg whites or 3/4 cup fat-free
cholesterol-free egg product for the eggs.

1 **SERVING:** Calories 280 (Calories from Fat 160); Fat 18g (Saturated 10g); Cholesterol 50mg;
Sodium 590mg; Carbohydrate 14g (Dietary Fiber 1g); Protein 16g • **% Daily Value:** Vitamin A 16%;
Vitamin C 6%; Calcium 32%; Iron 6% • **Exchanges:** 1/2 Starch, 1/2 Milk, 1 1/2 Medium-Fat Meat, 2 Fat •
Carbohydrate Choices: 1

High Altitude (3500 to 6500 feet): Use 1 1/4 cups milk. Bake 30 to 35 minutes.

Impossibly Easy
Southwestern Pie

Prep: **15 min** Bake: **40 min** Stand: **5 min**

6 servings

1 1/2 cups frozen whole kernel corn (from 1-pound bag)

8 medium green onions, chopped (1/2 cup)

1 can (15 ounces) black beans, rinsed and drained

1/3 cup shredded Cheddar cheese

1/2 cup Original Bisquick mix

1/2 cup milk

1/2 cup thick-and-chunky salsa

2 eggs

1 Heat oven to 400°. Spray pie plate, 9 × 1 1/4 inches, with cooking spray. Layer corn, onions and beans in pie plate; stir gently. Sprinkle with cheese.

2 Stir remaining ingredients in medium bowl with wire whisk or fork until blended. Pour into pie plate.

3 Bake 35 to 40 minutes or until knife inserted in center comes out clean. Let stand 5 minutes before serving. Serve with additional salsa if desired.

1 SERVING: Calories 225 (Calories from Fat 55); Fat 6g (Saturated 3g); Cholesterol 80mg; Sodium 580mg; Carbohydrate 36g (Dietary Fiber 6g); Protein 13g • **% Daily Value:** Vitamin A 10%; Vitamin C 6%; Calcium 16%; Iron 16% • **Exchanges:** 2 1/2 Starch, 1/2 Lean Meat • **Carbohydrate Choices:** 2 1/2

High Altitude (3500 to 6500 feet): Use 2/3 cup Bisquick mix. Bake 40 to 45 minutes.

Impossibly Easy
Green Bean Pie

Prep: **15 min** Bake: **35 min** Stand: **5 min**

6 servings

2 1/2 cups frozen
cut green beans
(from 1-pound bag),
thawed and drained

1 can (4 ounces)
mushroom pieces
and stems, drained

1 medium onion,
chopped (1/2 cup)

1 clove garlic, finely
chopped

1 cup shredded
Cheddar cheese
(4 ounces)

1/2 cup Original
Bisquick mix

1 cup milk

1/2 teaspoon salt

1/4 teaspoon pepper

2 eggs

1 Heat oven to 400°. Spray pie plate,
9 × 1 1/4 inches, with cooking spray.
Stir together beans, mushrooms,
onion, garlic and cheese in pie plate.

2 Stir remaining ingredients in medium
bowl with wire whisk or fork until
blended. Pour into pie plate, gently
stirring bean mixture.

3 Bake 30 to 35 minutes or until knife
inserted in center comes out clean.
Let stand 5 minutes before serving.

Reduced-Fat Impossibly Easy Green Bean Pie:
Use shredded reduced-fat Cheddar cheese,
Reduced Fat Bisquick mix and fat-free (skim)
milk. Substitute 3 egg whites or 1/2 cup fat-free
cholesterol-free egg product for the eggs.

1 SERVING: Calories 185 (Calories from Fat 90); Fat 10g (Saturated 5g); Cholesterol 95mg;
Sodium 580mg; Carbohydrate 14g (Dietary Fiber 2g); Protein 10g • **% Daily Value:** Vitamin A 12%;
Vitamin C 2%; Calcium 20%; Iron 6% • **Exchanges:** 1/2 Starch, 1 Vegetable, 1 High-Fat Meat, 1/2 Fat •
Carbohydrate Choices: 1

High Altitude (3500 to 6500 feet): Bake 37 to 42 minutes.

Impossibly Easy
Spinach Pie

(See photo insert)

Prep: **20 min** Bake: **35 min** Stand: **5 min**

6 servings

1 tablespoon butter or margarine

8 medium green onions, sliced (1/2 cup)

2 cloves garlic, finely chopped

1 package (9 ounces) frozen chopped spinach, thawed and squeezed to drain

1/2 cup small curd creamed cottage cheese

1/2 cup Original Bisquick mix

1 cup milk

1 teaspoon lemon juice

1/4 teaspoon pepper

3 eggs

3 tablespoons grated Parmesan cheese

1/4 teaspoon ground nutmeg

1 Heat oven to 350°. Spray pie plate, 9 × 1 1/4 inches, with cooking spray. Melt butter in 10-inch skillet over medium heat. Cook onions and garlic in butter 2 to 3 minutes, stirring occasionally, until onions are tender. Stir in spinach. Spread spinach mixture in pie plate. Spread with cottage cheese.

2 Stir Bisquick mix, milk, lemon juice, pepper and eggs in medium bowl with wire whisk or fork until blended. Pour into pie plate. Sprinkle with Parmesan cheese and nutmeg.

3 Bake about 35 minutes or until knife inserted in center comes out clean. Let stand 5 minutes before serving. Sprinkle with additional sliced green onions if desired.

1 SERVING: Calories 150 (Calories from Fat 70); Fat 8g (Saturated 3g); Cholesterol 115mg; Sodium 360mg; Carbohydrate 11g (Dietary Fiber 1g); Protein 10g • % **Daily Value:** Vitamin A 32%; Vitamin C 4%; Calcium 18%; Iron 6% • **Exchanges:** 2 Vegetable, 1 Lean Meat, 1 Fat • **Carbohydrate Choices:** 1

High Altitude (3500 to 6500 feet): Bake 35 to 40 minutes.

Impossibly Easy
Greek Spinach and Feta Pie

Prep: **10 min** Bake: **35 min** Stand: **5 min**

6 servings

1 package (9 ounces) frozen chopped spinach, thawed and squeezed to drain

1/2 cup crumbled feta cheese

4 medium green onions, sliced (1/4 cup)

1/2 cup Original Bisquick mix

2/3 cup milk

1/4 teaspoon salt

1/8 teaspoon pepper

2 eggs

1 Heat oven to 400°. Spray pie plate, 9 × 1 1/4 inches, with cooking spray. Stir together spinach, cheese and onions in pie plate.

2 Stir remaining ingredients in medium bowl with wire whisk or fork until blended. Pour into pie plate.

3 Bake 30 to 35 minutes or until knife inserted in center comes out clean. Let stand 5 minutes before serving.

1 SERVING: Calories 120 (Calories from Fat 55); Fat 6g (Saturated 3g); Cholesterol 85mg; Sodium 440mg; Carbohydrate 10g (Dietary Fiber 1g); Protein 7g • **% Daily Value:** Vitamin A 30%; Vitamin C 4%; Calcium 16%; Iron 6% • **Exchanges:** 1 Vegetable, 1/2 Milk, 1 Fat • **Carbohydrate Choices:** 1/2

High Altitude (3500 to 6500 feet): No changes.

Impossibly Easy

Zucchini Pie

(See photo insert)

Prep: 15 min   Bake: 35 min   Stand: 5 min

6 servings

1 small zucchini, chopped (1 cup)

1 large tomato, chopped (1 cup)

1 medium onion, chopped (1/2 cup)

1/2 cup Original Bisquick mix

1/3 cup grated Parmesan cheese

1 cup milk

1/2 teaspoon salt

1/8 teaspoon pepper

2 eggs

1 Heat oven to 400°. Spray pie plate, 9 × 1 1/4 inches, with cooking spray. Layer zucchini, tomato and onion in pie plate.

2 Stir remaining ingredients in medium bowl with wire whisk or fork until blended. Pour into pie plate.

3 Bake about 35 minutes or until knife inserted in center comes out clean. Let stand 5 minutes before serving.

Reduced-Fat Impossibly Easy Zucchini Pie: Use 2/3 cup Reduced Fat Bisquick mix and 3/4 cup fat-free (skim) milk. Substitute 3 egg whites or 1/2 cup fat-free cholesterol-free egg product for the eggs.

Impossibly Easy Double-Cheese Zucchini Pie: After layering zucchini, tomato and onion in pie plate, sprinkle with 1 cup shredded Swiss cheese (4 ounces). Continue as directed.

1 SERVING: Calories 130 (Calories from Fat 55); Fat 6g (Saturated 2g); Cholesterol 80mg; Sodium 490mg; Carbohydrate 12g (Dietary Fiber 1g); Protein 7g • **% Daily Value:** Vitamin A 12%; Vitamin C 6%; Calcium 16%; Iron 4% • **Exchanges:** 1/2 Starch, 1 Vegetable, 1/2 Medium-Fat Meat, 1/2 Fat • **Carbohydrate Choices:** 1

High Altitude (3500 to 6500 feet): Use 3/4 cup Bisquick mix. Bake 35 to 40 minutes.

Impossibly Easy
Peas and Rice Pie

Prep: **10 min** Bake: **28 min**

6 servings

1 cup water

1/2 teaspoon salt

1 cup uncooked
instant rice

2 tablespoons butter
or margarine,
softened

2 teaspoons instant
minced onion

3/4 cup frozen early
June peas (from
1-pound bag)

1/2 cup Original
Bisquick mix

1/2 cup grated
Parmesan cheese

1 cup milk

2 eggs

1/8 teaspoon pepper

1 Heat oven to 400°. Spray pie plate, 9 × 1 1/4 inches, with cooking spray.

2 Heat water and salt to boiling in 2-quart saucepan; remove from heat and stir in rice. Cover and let stand 5 minutes.

3 Stir butter, onion and peas into rice. Spoon into pie plate.

4 Stir remaining ingredients in medium bowl with wire whisk or fork until blended. Pour into pie plate.

5 Bake 24 to 28 minutes or until knife inserted in center comes out clean. Sprinkle with additional grated Parmesan cheese if desired.

1 SERVING: Calories 240 (Calories from Fat 90); Fat 10g (Saturated 5g); Cholesterol 90mg; Sodium 570mg; Carbohydrate 27g (Dietary Fiber 1g); Protein 10g • **% Daily Value:** Vitamin A 8%; Vitamin C 2%; Calcium 20%; Iron 8% • **Exchanges:** 2 Starch, 1 Medium-Fat Meat • **Carbohydrate Choices:** 2

High Altitude (3500 to 6500 feet): Bake 27 to 32 minutes.

Impossibly Easy

Ratatouille Pie

Prep: **15 min** Bake: **35 min** Stand: **5 min**

6 servings

1/4 cup butter or margarine

3/4 cup chopped zucchini

3/4 cup chopped peeled eggplant

1/4 cup chopped green bell pepper

1/4 cup finely chopped onion

1 small tomato, seeded and chopped (1/2 cup)

1 clove garlic, finely chopped

1/2 teaspoon dried basil leaves

1/2 teaspoon dried thyme leaves

1/2 teaspoon salt

1/8 teaspoon pepper

1 cup shredded Monterey Jack cheese (4 ounces)

1/2 cup Original Bisquick mix

1/4 cup sour cream

3/4 cup milk

2 eggs

1 Heat oven to 350°. Spray pie plate, 9 × 1 1/4 inches, with cooking spray.

2 Melt butter in 10-inch skillet over medium heat. Cook zucchini, eggplant, bell pepper, onion, tomato and garlic in butter 4 to 5 minutes, stirring occasionally, until vegetables are crisp-tender. Stir in basil, thyme, salt and pepper. Spread vegetable mixture in pie plate. Sprinkle with cheese.

3 Stir remaining ingredients in medium bowl with wire whisk or fork until blended. Pour into pie plate.

4 Bake 28 to 35 minutes or until knife inserted in center comes out clean and edge is golden brown. Let stand 5 minutes before serving.

1 SERVING: Calories 250 (Calories from Fat 170); Fat 19g (Saturated 11g); Cholesterol 115mg; Sodium 530mg; Carbohydrate 11g (Dietary Fiber 1g); Protein 9g • **% Daily Value:** Vitamin A 18%; Vitamin C 8%; Calcium 22%; Iron 4% • **Exchanges:** 1/2 Starch, 1 Vegetable, 1 High-Fat Meat, 2 Fat • **Carbohydrate Choices:** 1

High Altitude (3500 to 6500 feet): Use 3/4 cup Bisquick mix. Bake 33 to 38 minutes.

6

Fantastic
Fruity Pies

★ = Favorite

Impossibly Easy

French Apple Pie

(See photo insert)

Prep: **20 min**   Bake: **45 min**   Cool: **5 min**

8 servings

Streusel (below)

3 cups sliced
peeled tart apples
(3 medium)

1 teaspoon ground
cinnamon

1/4 teaspoon
ground nutmeg

1/2 cup Original
Bisquick mix

1/2 cup granulated
sugar

1/2 cup milk

1 tablespoon butter
or margarine,
softened

2 eggs

1 Heat oven to 325°. Spray pie plate,
9 × 1 1/4 inches, with cooking spray.
Make Streusel; set aside. Stir together
apples, cinnamon and nutmeg in medium
bowl. Spread in pie plate.

2 Stir remaining ingredients in medium
bowl with wire whisk or fork until
blended. Pour into pie plate. Sprinkle
with Streusel.

3 Bake 40 to 45 minutes or until knife
inserted in center comes out clean and
top is golden brown. Cool 5 minutes.
Serve warm or cool. Store covered in
refrigerator.

Streusel

1/2 cup Original
Bisquick mix

1/4 cup packed
brown sugar

1/4 cup chopped
nuts

2 tablespoons firm
butter or margarine

Stir together Bisquick mix, brown sugar and
nuts in small bowl. Cut in butter, using pastry
blender or crisscrossing 2 knives, until
crumbly.

Crowd-Size Impossibly Easy French Apple Pie:
Double all ingredients. Spray 13 × 9 × 2-inch
baking dish with cooking spray. Stir apple mixture and Bisquick mixture in large bowl. Bake
50 to 60 minutes.

1 **SERVING:** Calories 285 (Calories from Fat 125); Fat 14g (Saturated 4g); Cholesterol 65mg;
Sodium 270mg; Carbohydrate 36g (Dietary Fiber 1g); Protein 4g • % Daily Value: Vitamin A 6%;
Vitamin C 0%; Calcium 6%; Iron 6% • **Exchanges:** 1 Starch, 1 Fruit, 1/2 Other Carbohydrate, 2 1/2 Fat •
Carbohydrate Choices: 2 1/2

High Altitude (3500 to 6500 feet): Heat oven to 375°.

Impossibly Easy
Sour Cream–Apple Pie

Prep: **20 min** Bake: **45 min**

8 servings

2 cups thinly sliced apples (2 medium)

1/2 cup raisins

1/2 cup sugar

1 teaspoon ground cinnamon

1/2 cup Original Bisquick mix

1/2 cup sour cream

1/3 cup half-and-half

2 tablespoons butter or margarine, melted

2 eggs

1/8 teaspoon ground cinnamon

1 Heat oven to 350°. Spray pie plate, 9 × 1 1/4 inches, with cooking spray. Stir together apples, raisins, sugar and 1 teaspoon cinnamon in pie plate.

2 Stir remaining ingredients except 1/8 teaspoon cinnamon in medium bowl with wire whisk or fork until blended. Pour into pie plate. Sprinkle with 1/8 teaspoon cinnamon.

3 Bake 40 to 45 minutes or until apples are tender and knife inserted in center comes out clean. Serve warm. Store covered in refrigerator.

Reduced-Fat Impossibly Easy Sour Cream–Apple Pie: Use Reduced Fat Bisquick mix and reduced-fat sour cream. Substitute 3 egg whites or 1/2 cup fat-free cholesterol-free egg product for the eggs.

1 SERVING: Calories 215 (Calories from Fat 80); Fat 9g (Saturated 5g); Cholesterol 75mg; Sodium 150mg; Carbohydrate 31g (Dietary Fiber 1g); Protein 3g • % **Daily Value:** Vitamin A 6%; Vitamin C 0%; Calcium 4%; Iron 4% • **Exchanges:** 1 Starch, 1/2 Fruit, 1/2 Other Carbohydrate, 2 Fat • **Carbohydrate Choices:** 2

High Altitude (3500 to 6500 feet): Bake 43 to 48 minutes.

Impossibly Easy
Apricot Pie

(See photo insert) Prep: **15 min** Bake: **40 min** Cool: **2 hr**

8 servings

1/2 cup Original Bisquick mix

1 cup evaporated milk (from 12-ounce can)

1/2 cup sugar

2 tablespoons butter or margarine, softened

1 teaspoon vanilla

2 eggs

1 can (8 1/2 ounces) apricot halves, drained and mashed*

1/4 cup apricot preserves

Sweetened Whipped Cream (page 147), if desired

1 Heat oven to 350°. Spray pie plate, 9 × 1 1/4 inches, with cooking spray.

2 Stir together all ingredients except preserves and Sweetened Whipped Cream in medium bowl with wire whisk or fork until blended. Pour into pie plate.

3 Bake 35 to 40 minutes or until knife inserted in center comes out clean. Cool completely, about 2 hours.

4 Melt preserves in 1-quart saucepan over low heat, stirring occasionally, until melted; spread over pie. Cool. Garnish with Sweetened Whipped Cream. Store covered in refrigerator.

Half of 1 can (15 ounces) apricot halves, drained and mashed, can be used instead of the 8 1/2-ounce can.

1 SERVING: Calories 205 (Calories from Fat 65); Fat 7g (Saturated 3g); Cholesterol 65mg; Sodium 180mg; Carbohydrate 31g (Dietary Fiber 1g); Protein 5g • % **Daily Value:** Vitamin A 70%; Vitamin C 2%; Calcium 10%; Iron 2% • **Exchanges:** 1 Starch, 1/2 Fruit, 1/2 Other Carbohydrate, 1 1/2 Fat • **Carbohydrate Choices:** 2

High Altitude (3500 to 6500 feet): No changes.

Impossibly Easy
Mixed–Berry Crumble Pie

Prep: **10 min** Bake: **1 hr**

8 servings

Streusel (below)

1 bag (12 ounces) frozen mixed berries (about 2 1/2 cups)

1 teaspoon ground cinnamon

1/4 teaspoon ground nutmeg

1/2 cup Original Bisquick mix

1/2 cup sugar

1/2 cup milk

1 tablespoon butter or margarine, softened

2 eggs

1 Heat oven to 325°. Spray pie plate, 9 × 1 1/4 inches, with cooking spray. Make Streusel; set aside. Mix frozen berries, cinnamon and nutmeg in medium bowl. Spread in pie plate.

2 Stir remaining ingredients in medium bowl with wire whisk or fork until blended. Pour into pie plate. Sprinkle with Streusel.

3 Bake 50 to 60 minutes or until top is evenly deep golden brown.

Streusel

1/2 cup Original Bisquick mix

1/4 cup packed brown sugar

1/4 cup chopped nuts

2 tablespoons firm butter or margarine

Mix Bisquick mix, brown sugar and nuts in small bowl. Cut in butter, using pastry blender or crisscrossing 2 knives, until crumbly.

Crowd-Size Impossibly Easy Mixed-Berry Crumble Pie: Double all ingredients. Spray 13 × 9 × 2-inch baking dish with cooking spray. Stir Bisquick mixture in large bowl. Bake 55 to 65 minutes.

1 SERVING: Calories 260 (Calories from Fat 100); Fat 11g (Saturated 4g); Cholesterol 65mg; Sodium 270mg; Carbohydrate 36g (Dietary Fiber 2g); Protein 4g • **% Daily Value:** Vitamin A 6%; Vitamin C 10%; Calcium 6%; Iron 6% • **Exchanges:** 1 Starch, 1 Fruit, 1/2 Other Carbohydrate, 2 Fat • Carbohydrate Choices: 2 1/2

High Altitude (3500 to 6500 feet): Heat oven to 350°. Bake 55 to 60 minutes.

Impossibly Easy
Cherry Custard Pie

Prep: **15 min** Bake: **40 min** Cool: **2 hr**

8 servings

1/2 cup Original Bisquick mix

1/4 cup granulated sugar

3/4 cup milk

2 tablespoons butter or margarine, softened

1/4 teaspoon almond extract

2 eggs

1 can (21 ounces) cherry pie filling, drained*

Cinnamon Streusel (below)

* Do not use blueberry pie filling.

1 Heat oven to 400°. Spray pie plate, 9 × 1 1/4 inches, with cooking spray.

2 Stir all ingredients except pie filling and Cinnamon Streusel in medium bowl with wire whisk or fork until blended. Pour into pie plate. Spoon pie filling evenly over top.

3 Bake 30 to 35 minutes or until knife inserted in center comes out clean. Meanwhile, make Cinnamon Streusel; sprinkle over pie. Bake about 5 minutes longer or until streusel is brown. Cool completely, about 2 hours. Store covered in refrigerator.

Cinnamon Streusel

1/4 cup Original Bisquick mix

1/4 cup packed brown sugar

1/4 teaspoon ground cinnamon

1 tablespoon firm butter or margarine

Stir together Bisquick mix, brown sugar and cinnamon in small bowl. Cut in butter, using pastry blender or crisscrossing 2 knives, until crumbly.

Reduced-Fat Impossibly Easy Cherry Custard Pie: Use Reduced Fat Bisquick mix and fat-free (skim) milk. Substitute 3 egg whites or 1/2 cup fat-free cholesterol-free egg product for the eggs.

1 SERVING: Calories 240 (Calories from Fat 70); Fat 8g (Saturated 4g); Cholesterol 65mg; Sodium 220mg; Carbohydrate 39g (Dietary Fiber 1g); Protein 3g • % Daily Value: Vitamin A 6%; Vitamin C 0%; Calcium 6%; Iron 4% • **Exchanges:** 1 Starch, 1/2 Fruit, 1 Other Carbohydrate, 1 1/2 Fat • **Carbohydrate Choices:** 2 1/2

High Altitude (3500 to 6500 feet): No changes.

Impossibly Easy

Cranberry–Orange Pie

Prep: **20 min** Bake: **40 min** Chill: **3 hr**

8 servings

1/2 cup chopped fresh or frozen cranberries

2 teaspoons grated orange peel

3/4 cup Original Bisquick mix

3/4 cup sugar

1 cup milk

3 tablespoons butter or margarine, melted

1/2 teaspoon vanilla

2 eggs

Sweetened Whipped Cream (page 147), if desired

1. Heat oven to 350°. Spray pie plate, 9 × 1 1/4 inches, with cooking spray. Stir together cranberries and orange peel in small bowl. Sprinkle evenly in pie plate.

2. Stir remaining ingredients except Sweetened Whipped Cream in medium bowl with wire whisk or fork until blended. Pour into pie plate.

3. Bake 35 to 40 minutes or until knife inserted in center comes out clean; cool. Refrigerate at least 3 hours but no longer than 24 hours. Garnish with Sweetened Whipped Cream. Store covered in refrigerator.

Reduced-Fat Impossibly Easy Cranberry-Orange Pie: Use Reduced Fat Bisquick mix, fat-free (skim) milk and fat-free whipped topping. Substitute 3 egg whites or 1/2 cup fat-free cholesterol-free egg product for the eggs.

1 SERVING: Calories 180 (Calories from Fat 55); Fat 6g (Saturated 3g); Cholesterol 65mg; Sodium 210mg; Carbohydrate 28g (Dietary Fiber 0g); Protein 3g • **% Daily Value:** Vitamin A 4%; Vitamin C 0%; Calcium 6%; Iron 2% • **Exchanges:** 1 Starch, 1 Other Carbohydrate, 1 Fat • **Carbohydrate Choices:** 2

High Altitude (3500 to 6500 feet): No changes.

Impossibly Easy
Lemon–
Macaroon Pie

Prep: **15 min** Bake: **35 min** Cool: **5 min**

8 servings

3/4 cup Original Bisquick mix

1 cup milk

1/2 cup sugar

2 tablespoons butter or margarine, softened

2 teaspoons grated lemon peel

2 tablespoons lemon juice

1 teaspoon vanilla

2 eggs

1/2 cup flaked coconut

1 Heat oven to 350°. Spray pie plate, 9 × 1 1/4 inches, with cooking spray.

2 Stir all ingredients except coconut in medium bowl with wire whisk or fork until blended. Pour into pie plate. Sprinkle with coconut.

3 Bake 30 to 35 minutes or until golden brown and knife inserted in center comes out clean. Cool 5 minutes. Store covered in refrigerator.

Reduced-Fat Impossibly Easy Lemon-Macaroon Pie: Use Reduced Fat Bisquick mix, and fat-free (skim) milk. Substitute 3 egg whites or 1/2 cup fat-free cholesterol-free egg product for the eggs.

1 SERVING: Calories 180 (Calories from Fat 70); Fat 8g (Saturated 4g); Cholesterol 65mg; Sodium 220mg; Carbohydrate 23g (Dietary Fiber 0g); Protein 4g • **% Daily Value:** Vitamin A 4%; Vitamin C 0%; Calcium 6%; Iron 2% • **Exchanges:** 1 Starch, 1/2 Other Carbohydrate, 1 1/2 Fat • **Carbohydrate Choices:** 1 1/2

High Altitude (3500 to 6500 feet): Bake 33 to 38 minutes.

Impossibly Easy
Fresh Peach
Streusel Pie

Prep: **15 min** Bake: **35 min**

8 servings

Streusel (below)

1/2 cup Original
Bisquick mix

1/3 cup granulated
sugar

3/4 cup milk

2 tablespoons butter
or margarine,
softened

2 eggs

3 cups sliced peeled
fresh peaches*

1 Heat oven to 400°. Spray pie plate,
9 × 1 1/4 inches, with cooking spray.
Make Streusel; set aside.

2 Stir remaining ingredients except
peaches in medium bowl with wire
whisk or fork until blended. Pour into
pie plate. Arrange peaches evenly over
top. Sprinkle with Streusel.

3 Bake 30 to 35 minutes or until knife
inserted in center comes out clean. Serve
warm. Store covered in refrigerator.

**1 bag (1 pound) frozen sliced peaches, thawed
and drained, can be used instead of the fresh
peaches.*

Streusel

1/4 cup Original
Bisquick mix

1/4 cup packed
brown sugar

1/4 teaspoon
ground cinnamon

1 tablespoon firm
butter or margarine

Stir together Bisquick mix, brown sugar and
cinnamon in small bowl. Cut in butter, using
pastry blender or crisscrossing 2 knives,
until crumbly.

1 SERVING: Calories 210 (Calories from Fat 70); Fat 8g (Saturated 4g); Cholesterol 65mg;
Sodium 220mg; Carbohydrate 30g (Dietary Fiber 1g); Protein 4g • % **Daily Value:** Vitamin A 8%;
Vitamin C 2%; Calcium 6%; Iron 4% • **Exchanges:** 1 Starch, 1 Fruit, 1 1/2 Fat • **Carbohydrate Choices:** 2

High Altitude (3500 to 6500 feet): Bake 38 to 43 minutes.

Peaches 'n Cream Pie

Prep: **20 min** Bake: **40 min**

8 servings

Almond Streusel (below)

2 cans (15 1/4 ounces each) sliced peaches, well drained, or 3 cups sliced fresh peaches

1/2 teaspoon ground cinnamon

1/4 teaspoon ground nutmeg

1/2 cup Original Bisquick mix

1/2 cup sugar

1 cup whipping (heavy) cream

2 eggs

Sweetened Whipped Cream (page 147), if desired

1 Heat oven to 375°. Spray pie plate, 9 × 1 1/4 inches, with cooking spray. Make Almond Streusel; set aside. Pat peach slices dry; place in pie plate. Sprinkle with cinnamon and nutmeg; toss. Spread evenly in pie plate.

2 Stir remaining ingredients except Sweetened Whipped Cream in medium bowl with wire whisk or fork until blended. Pour into pie plate, lifting ingredients to allow mixture to flow into pie plate. Sprinkle with streusel.

3 Bake 35 to 40 minutes or until knife inserted in center comes out clean. Serve with Sweetened Whipped Cream. Serve warm or cold. Store covered in refrigerator.

Almond Streusel

1/4 cup Original Bisquick mix

2 tablespoons sugar

1 tablespoon firm butter or margarine

1/3 cup slivered almonds

Stir together Bisquick mix and sugar in small bowl. Cut in butter, using pastry blender or crisscrossing 2 knives, until crumbly. Stir in almonds.

1 SERVING: Calories 310 (Calories from Fat 145); Fat 16g (Saturated 8g); Cholesterol 90mg; Sodium 200mg; Carbohydrate 37g (Dietary Fiber 2g); Protein 4g • **% Daily Value:** Vitamin A 24%; Vitamin C 2%; Calcium 6%; Iron 6% • **Exchanges:** 1 Starch, 1 1/2 Other Carbohydrate, 3 Fat • **Carbohydrate Choices:** 2 1/2

High Altitude (3500 to 6500 feet): Use 2/3 cup Bisquick mix in pie. Cut each peach slice into thirds.

Impossibly Easy
Pumpkin Pie

Prep: **10 min** Bake: **40 min** Cool: **2 hr**

8 servings

1 cup canned
pumpkin (not
pumpkin pie mix)

1/2 cup Original
Bisquick mix

1/2 cup sugar

1 cup evaporated
milk (from 12-ounce
can)

1 tablespoon butter
or margarine,
softened

1 1/2 teaspoons
pumpkin pie spice*

1 teaspoon vanilla

2 eggs

Spiced Whipped
Topping (below)

1 Heat oven to 350°. Spray pie plate,
9 × 1 1/4 inches, with cooking spray.

2 Stir all ingredients except Spiced
Whipped Topping in medium bowl with
wire whisk or fork until blended. Pour
into pie plate.

3 Bake 35 to 40 minutes or until knife
inserted in center comes out clean. Cool
2 hours. Serve with Spiced Whipped
Topping. Store covered in refrigerator.

**1 teaspoon each ground cinnamon, ground
nutmeg and ground ginger can be used instead
of the pumpkin pie spice in the pie.*

Spiced Whipped Topping

1 1/2 cups frozen
(thawed) whipped
topping

1/4 teaspoon
pumpkin pie spice

Stir all ingredients in small bowl until smooth.

Crowd-Size Impossibly Easy Pumpkin Pie:
Double all ingredients. Spray 13 × 9 × 2-inch
baking dish with cooking spray. Stir Bisquick
mixture in large bowl. Bake 36 to 46 minutes.

Impossibly Easy Sweet Potato Pie: Substitute
1 cup canned sweet potatoes for the pumpkin.
Drain sweet potatoes if necessary; mash with
food processor or fork.

1 SERVING: Calories 195 (Calories from Fat 70); Fat 8g (Saturated 3g); Cholesterol 60mg;
Sodium 170mg; Carbohydrate 26g (Dietary Fiber 1g); Protein 5g • **% Daily Value:** Vitamin A 100%;
Vitamin C 0%; Calcium 12%; Iron 4% • **Exchanges:** 1 1/2 Starch, 1/2 Other Carbohydrate, 1 Fat •
Carbohydrate Choices: 2

High Altitude (3500 to 6500 feet): Heat oven to 375°.

Impossibly Easy
Piña Colada Pie

Prep: **10 min** Bake: **40 min** Cool: **10 min**

8 servings

1 cup canned cream of coconut (not coconut milk)

3/4 cup flaked coconut

1/2 cup Original Bisquick mix

1/4 cup milk

1/4 cup rum*

1 tablespoon butter or margarine, softened

2 eggs

1 can (8 ounces) crushed pineapple in juice, well drained

1/2 cup flaked coconut

Sweetened Whipped Cream (page 147), if desired

1 Heat oven to 350°. Spray pie plate, 9 × 1 1/4 inches, with cooking spray.

2 Stir all ingredients except 1/2 cup coconut and Sweetened Whipped Cream in medium bowl with wire whisk or fork until blended. Pour into pie plate. Sprinkle with 1/2 cup coconut.

3 Bake 30 to 40 minutes or until knife inserted in center comes out clean. Cool 10 minutes. Garnish with Sweetened Whipped Cream. Store covered in refrigerator.

*2 teaspoons rum extract plus 2 tablespoons milk can be used instead of the rum.

Reduced-Fat Impossibly Easy Piña Colada Pie: Use Reduced Fat Bisquick mix and fat-free (skim) milk. Substitute 3 egg whites or 1/2 cup fat-free cholesterol-free egg product for the eggs.

1 SERVING: Calories 245 (Calories from Fat 160); Fat 18g (Saturated 15g); Cholesterol 55mg; Sodium 170mg; Carbohydrate 17g (Dietary Fiber 2g); Protein 4g • % Daily Value: Vitamin A 2%; Vitamin C 2%; Calcium 4%; Iron 8% • **Exchanges:** 1 Starch, 3 1/2 Fat • **Carbohydrate Choices:** 1

High Altitude (3500 to 6500 feet): Bake 35 to 40 minutes.

Impossibly Easy

Rhubarb Streusel Pie

Prep: **15 min** Bake: **40 min**

8 servings

Streusel Topping (below)

2 cups 1/2-inch pieces fresh rhubarb

1 cup granulated sugar

1/2 cup Original Bisquick mix

3/4 cup milk

2 tablespoons butter or margarine, softened

1 teaspoon ground cinnamon

1/4 teaspoon ground nutmeg

2 eggs

Sweetened Whipped Cream (page 147), if desired

1 Heat oven to 375°. Spray pie plate, 9 × 1 1/4 inches, with cooking spray. Make Streusel Topping; set aside. Spread rhubarb evenly in pie plate.

2 Stir remaining ingredients except Sweetened Whipped Cream in medium bowl with wire whisk or fork until blended. Pour into pie plate. Sprinkle topping evenly over top.

3 Bake about 40 minutes or until knife inserted in center comes out clean. Serve warm with Sweetened Whipped Cream. Store covered in refrigerator.

Streusel Topping

1/2 cup Original Bisquick mix

1/4 cup packed brown sugar

1/4 cup chopped nuts

2 tablespoons firm butter or margarine

Stir together Bisquick mix, brown sugar and nuts in small bowl. Cut in butter, using pastry blender or crisscrossing 2 knives, until crumbly.

1 SERVING: Calories 295 (Calories from Fat 110); Fat 12g (Saturated 5g); Cholesterol 70mg; Sodium 280mg; Carbohydrate 43g (Dietary Fiber 1g); Protein 4g • % **Daily Value:** Vitamin A 6%; Vitamin C 0%; Calcium 12%; Iron 6% • **Exchanges:** 1 Starch, 2 Other Carbohydrate, 2 Fat • **Carbohydrate Choices:** 3

High Altitude (3500 to 6500 feet): Use 3/4 cup Bisquick mix in pie.

7

Sweet-Tooth Temptations

⭐ = Favorite

Impossibly Easy
Cheesecake

(See photo insert)

Prep: **10 min** Bake: **37 min** Cool: **1 hr**
Chill: **8 hr**

8 servings

1/2 cup milk

2 teaspoons vanilla

2 eggs

3/4 cup sugar

1/4 cup Original
Bisquick mix

2 packages (8 ounces
each) cream cheese,
cut into 16 pieces
and softened

Sour Cream
Topping (below)

Fresh berries
or sliced fruit,
if desired

1 Heat oven to 325°. Spray pie plate,
9 × 1 1/4 inches, with cooking spray.

2 Place milk, vanilla, eggs, sugar and
Bisquick mix in blender. Cover and
blend on high speed 15 seconds. Add
cream cheese. Cover and blend 2 minutes. Pour into pie plate.

3 Bake 27 to 37 minutes or until edge is
just beginning to crack and center is
still shiny and soft and wiggles slightly.
Cool completely, about 1 hour. Spread
Sour Cream Topping over top of cooled
cheesecake. Refrigerate at least 8 hours.
Garnish with berries. Store covered in
refrigerator.

Sour Cream Topping

1 cup sour cream

2 tablespoons sugar

2 teaspoons vanilla

Stir all ingredients in small bowl until blended.

Crowd-Size Impossibly Easy Cheesecake:
Double all ingredients. Spray 13 × 9 × 2-inch
baking dish with cooking spray. Beat all ingredients except Sour Cream Topping and berries in
large bowl with electric mixer on high speed
about 2 minutes, scraping bowl frequently, until
smooth. Bake 32 to 42 minutes.

1 SERVING: Calories 390 (Calories from Fat 250); Fat 28g (Saturated 17g); Cholesterol 135mg;
Sodium 255mg; Carbohydrate 28g (Dietary Fiber 0g); Protein 8g • **% Daily Value:** Vitamin A 22%;
Vitamin C 0%; Calcium 12%; Iron 4% • **Exchanges:** 1 Starch, 1 Other Carbohydrate, 1/2 High-Fat Meat,
4 1/2 Fat • **Carbohydrate Choices:** 2

High Altitude (3500 to 6500 feet): Heat oven to 350°. Bake 30 to 35 minutes.

Impossibly Easy
Cherry
Cheesecake

Prep: **11 min** Bake: **35 min** Cool: **1 hr**
Chill: **3 hr**

8 servings

1/3 cup milk

1 teaspoon vanilla

1 egg

1/2 cup sugar

1/4 cup Original
Bisquick mix

1 package (8 ounces)
cream cheese, cut
into 16 pieces and
softened

Sour Cream
Topping (left)

1 cup cherry
preserves

1 Heat oven to 350°. Spray pie plate,
9 × 1 1/4 inches, with cooking spray.

2 Place milk, vanilla, egg, sugar and
Bisquick mix in blender. Cover and
blend on high speed 15 seconds. Add
cream cheese. Cover and blend 1 minute. Pour into pie plate.

3 Bake 30 to 35 minutes or until center
is firm. Cool completely, about 1 hour.
Spread Sour Cream Topping over top
of cooled cheesecake. Refrigerate at
least 3 hours. Serve with preserves.
Store covered in refrigerator.

**Reduced-Fat Impossibly Easy Cherry Cheese-
cake:** Substitute 2 egg whites or 1/4 cup fat-
free cholesterol-free egg product for the egg.
Use Reduced Fat Bisquick mix and reduced-fat
cream cheese (Neufchâtel). Use reduced-fat
sour cream in Sour Cream Topping.

1 SERVING: Calories 325 (Calories from Fat 125); Fat 14g (Saturated 8g); Cholesterol 70mg;
Sodium 170mg; Carbohydrate 46g (Dietary Fiber 0g); Protein 4g • % Daily Value: Vitamin A 10%;
Vitamin C 2%; Calcium 6%; Iron 4% • **Exchanges:** 1/2 Starch, 1/2 Fruit, 2 Other Carbohydrate, 3 Fat •
Carbohydrate Choices: 3

High Altitude (3500 to 6500 feet): Bake 32 to 37 minutes.

Impossibly Easy
Chocolate
Cheesecake

Prep: **10 min** Bake: **30 min** Cool: **1 hr**
Chill: **3 hr**

8 servings

3/4 cup sugar

1/2 cup Original
Bisquick mix

1/4 cup baking
cocoa

2 eggs

2 packages (8 ounces
each) cream cheese,
cut into 16 pieces
and softened

2 teaspoons vanilla

Sour Cream Topping
(page 136)

1 Heat oven to 350°. Spray pie plate,
9 × 1 1/4 inches, with cooking spray.

2 Place all ingredients except desired
Topping in blender. Cover and blend
on high speed about 3 minutes, stopping blender occasionally to stir, until
smooth. (Or beat in large bowl with
electric mixer on high speed 2 minutes, scraping bowl constantly.) Pour
into pie plate.

3 Bake about 30 minutes or just until
puffed and center is dry (do not over-
bake). Spread Sour Cream Topping
carefully over top of warm cheesecake;
cool completely, about 1 hour. Store
covered in refrigerator.

1 SERVING: Calories 550 (Calories from Fat 360); Fat 40g (Saturated 22g); Cholesterol 200mg;
Sodium 340mg; Carbohydrate 38g (Dietary Fiber 2g); Protein 10g • **% Daily Value:** Vitamin A 26%;
Vitamin C 0%; Calcium 12%; Iron 10% • **Exchanges:** 2 Starch, 1/2 Other Carbohydrate, 8 Fat •
Carbohydrate Choices: 2 1/2

High Altitude (3500 to 6500 feet): Add 1/4 cup milk to blended ingredients. Bake 30 to 35 minutes.

138

Impossibly Easy

Mocha Fudge Cheesecake

(See photo insert)

Prep: **10 min** Bake: **35 min** Cool: **1 hr 5 min**
Chill: **3 hr**

8 servings

1 tablespoon
instant coffee (dry)

3 tablespoons coffee
liqueur or cold
strong brewed coffee

2 packages (8 ounces
each) cream cheese,
cut into 16 pieces
and softened

3/4 cup Original
Bisquick mix

3/4 cup sugar

1 teaspoon vanilla

3 eggs

3 ounces semisweet
baking chocolate,
melted and cooled

Chocolate Topping
(below)

1 Heat oven to 350°. Spray pie plate,
9 × 1 1/4 inches, with cooking spray.
Stir coffee and liqueur in small bowl
until coffee is dissolved.

2 Beat coffee mixture and remaining
ingredients except Chocolate Topping
in large bowl with electric mixer on
high speed about 2 minutes, until well
blended. Pour into pie plate.

3 Bake about 35 minutes or until center
is firm and puffed. Cool 5 minutes (top
of cheesecake will be cracked). Carefully spread Chocolate Topping over
cheesecake. Cool completely, about
1 hour. Refrigerate at least 3 hours
until chilled. Store covered in refrigerator.

Chocolate Topping

1 ounce semisweet
baking chocolate,
melted and cooled

2 tablespoons
powdered sugar

1 container (8 ounces)
sour cream

1 teaspoon vanilla

Stir all ingredients in small bowl until
blended.

1 SERVING: Calories 490 (Calories from Fat 295); Fat 33g (Saturated 19g); Cholesterol 160mg;
Sodium 360mg; Carbohydrate 40g (Dietary Fiber 1g); Protein 9g • **% Daily Value:** Vitamin A 24%;
Vitamin C 0%; Calcium 10%; Iron 10% • **Exchanges:** 1 Starch, 1 1/2 Other Carbohydrate, 1/2 High-Fat
Meat, 6 Fat • **Carbohydrate Choices:** 2 1/2

High Altitude (3500 to 6500 feet): Bake about 40 minutes.

Impossibly Easy

Chocolate-and-Almond-Topped Cheesecake

Prep: **15 min** Bake: **47 min** Cool: **1 hr**
Chill: **3 hr**

8 servings

3/4 cup milk

1 teaspoon vanilla

1 teaspoon almond extract

2 eggs

1 cup sugar

1/2 cup Original Bisquick mix

2 packages (8 ounces each) cream cheese, cut into 16 pieces and softened

1/2 cup semisweet chocolate chips

1/2 cup toasted chopped almonds

1 Heat oven to 350°. Spray pie plate, 9 × 1 1/4 inches, with cooking spray.

2 Place milk, vanilla, almond extract, eggs, sugar and Bisquick mix in blender. Cover and blend on high speed 15 seconds. Add cream cheese. Cover and blend 2 minutes. Pour into pie plate.

3 Bake 40 to 45 minutes or until center is firm. Immediately sprinkle with chocolate chips. Bake about 2 minutes longer or until chocolate is melted. Spread chocolate evenly; sprinkle with almonds. Cool completely, about 1 hour. Refrigerate at least 3 hours until chilled. Store covered in refrigerator.

1 SERVING: Calories 465 (Calories from Fat 270); Fat 30g (Saturated 16g); Cholesterol 115mg; Sodium 300mg; Carbohydrate 40g (Dietary Fiber 2g); Protein 9g • % Daily Value: Vitamin A 18%; Vitamin C 0%; Calcium 12%; Iron 10% • Exchanges: 2 Starch, 1/2 Other Carbohydrate, 6 Fat • **Carbohydrate Choices: 2 1/2**

High Altitude (3500 to 6500 feet): Bake 45 to 50 minutes.

Impossibly Easy

Pumpkin Cheesecake

Prep: **10 min** Bake: **45 min** Cool: **1 hr**
Chill: **3 hr**

8 servings

1 can (15 ounces) pumpkin (not pumpkin pie mix)

1 package (8 ounces) cream cheese, cut into 16 pieces and softened

1/4 teaspoon vanilla

3 eggs

3/4 cup sugar

1/2 cup Original Bisquick mix

1 1/2 teaspoons pumpkin pie spice

Pecan halves, if desired

1 Heat oven to 350°. Spray pie plate, 9 × 1 1/4 inches, with cooking spray.

2 Place all ingredients except pecan halves in blender. Cover and blend on high speed about 2 minutes or until smooth. (Or beat in medium bowl with wire whisk or hand beater 2 minutes.) Pour into pie plate.

3 Bake about 45 minutes or just until puffed and center is dry (do not over-bake). Cool completely, about 1 hour. Refrigerate at least 3 hours until chilled. Garnish with pecan halves. Store covered in refrigerator.

Impossibly Easy Sweet Potato Cheesecake: Substitute 2 cups mashed cooked sweet potatoes for the pumpkin.

1 **SERVING:** Calories 430 (Calories from Fat 225); Fat 25g (Saturated 14g); Cholesterol 170mg; Sodium 300mg; Carbohydrates 44g (Dietary Fiber 2g); Protein 9g • % **Daily Value:** Vitamin A 100%; Vitamin C 2%; Calcium 12%; Iron 12% • **Exchanges:** 1 Starch, 2 Other Carbohydrate, 5 Fat • **Carbohydrate Choices:** 3

High Altitude (3500 to 6500 feet): No changes.

Impossibly Easy

Fresh Lime
Cheesecake

Prep: **10 min** Bake: **37 min** Cool: **1 hr**
Chill: **8 hr**

8 servings

1 tablespoon grated lime peel

1/4 cup milk

2 eggs

3/4 cup sugar

1/4 cup Original Bisquick mix

2 packages (8 ounces each) cream cheese, softened and cut into 16 pieces

1/4 cup fresh lime juice

1 1/2 cups frozen (thawed) whipped topping

Additional 1 tablespoon grated lime peel, if desired

1 Heat oven to 325°. Spray pie plate, 9 × 1 1/4 inches, with cooking spray.

2 Place lime peel, milk, eggs, sugar and Bisquick mix in blender or food processor. Cover and blend on high speed 15 seconds. Add cream cheese; cover and blend about 2 minutes or until smooth. Add lime juice; cover and blend 10 to 15 seconds or until well mixed. Pour into pie plate.

3 Bake 27 to 37 minutes or until edge is just beginning to crack and center is still shiny and soft and wiggles slightly.

4 Cool 1 hour. Cover and refrigerate at least 8 hours.

5 Run knife around edge of pie plate to loosen cheesecake if necessary. Spread whipped topping over cheesecake. Sprinkle with additional lime peel.

1 SERVING: Calories 350 (Calories from Fat 215); Fat 24g (Saturated 14g); Cholesterol 115mg; Sodium 240mg; Carbohydrate 26g (Dietary Fiber 0g); Protein 7g • **% Daily Value:** Vitamin A 18%; Vitamin C 4%; Calcium 6%; Iron 4% • **Exchanges:** 1 Starch, 1 Other Carbohydrate, 4 1/2 Fat • **Carbohydrate Choices:** 2

High Altitude (3500 to 6500 feet): Heat oven to 350°. Bake 30 to 35 minutes.

Grasshopper Cheesecake

(See photo insert)

Prep: **8 min** Bake: **35 min** Cool: **45 min**
Chill: **3 hr**

10 to 12 servings

3/4 cup Original Bisquick mix

3/4 cup sugar

1/4 cup green crème de menthe

3 eggs

2 packages (8 ounces each) cream cheese, softened

1/4 cup miniature semisweet chocolate chips

Chocolate Ganache (below)

1 Heat oven to 350°. Spray pie plate, 9 × 1 1/4 inches, with cooking spray.

2 Beat all ingredients except chocolate chips and Chocolate Ganache in large bowl with electric mixer on high speed 2 minutes, scraping bowl frequently. Stir in chocolate chips. Pour into pie plate.

3 Bake about 35 minutes or until center is firm and puffed. Cool 45 minutes (cheesecake top will be cracked). Carefully spread Chocolate Ganache over cheesecake. Refrigerate at least 3 hours until chilled. Store covered in refrigerator.

Chocolate Ganache

1/2 cup whipping (heavy) cream

1 cup miniature semisweet chocolate chips

Heat ingredients in 1-quart saucepan over medium heat, stirring constantly, until smooth; remove from heat.

Crowd-Size Impossibly Easy Grasshopper Cheesecake: Double all ingredients. Spray 13 × 9 × 2-inch baking dish with cooking spray. Bake 30 to 37 minutes.

1 SERVING: Calories 430 (Calories from Fat 260); Fat 29g (Saturated 17g); Cholesterol 125mg; Sodium 290mg; Carbohydrate 37g (Dietary Fiber 1g); Protein 7g • % Daily Value: Vitamin A 16%; Vitamin C 0%; Calcium 6%; Iron 8% • **Exchanges:** 2 Starch, 1/2 Other Carbohydrate, 5 1/2 Fat • **Carbohydrate Choices:** 2 1/2

High Altitude (3500 to 6500 feet): No changes.

Impossibly Easy
Brownie Pie

Prep: **15 min** Bake: **35 min** Cool: **1 hr**

8 servings

4 eggs

1/4 cup butter or margarine, melted

4 ounces sweet baking chocolate, melted and cooled

1/2 cup packed brown sugar

1/2 cup Original Bisquick mix

1/2 cup granulated sugar

3/4 cup chopped nuts

Ice cream or Sweetened Whipped Cream (page 147), if desired

1 Heat oven to 350°. Spray pie plate, 9 × 1 1/4 inches, with cooking spray.

2 If using blender: Place eggs, butter and chocolate in blender. Cover and blend on high speed about 10 seconds or until smooth. Add brown sugar, Bisquick mix and granulated sugar. Cover and blend on high speed 1 minute, stopping blender occasionally to scrape sides. If using hand beater: Beat eggs, butter and chocolate in medium bowl with hand beater about 30 seconds or until smooth. Add brown sugar, Bisquick mix and granulated sugar. Beat 2 minutes.

3 Pour batter into pie plate. Sprinkle with nuts. Bake about 35 minutes or until knife inserted in center comes out clean. Cool completely, about 1 hour. Serve with ice cream.

1 SERVING: Calories 395 (Calories from Fat 225); Fat 25g (Saturated 10g); Cholesterol 120mg; Sodium 180mg; Carbohydrate 36g (Dietary Fiber 3g); Protein 6g • % **Daily Value:** Vitamin A 8%; Vitamin C 0%; Calcium 6%; Iron 10% • **Exchanges:** 2 Starch, 1/2 Other Carbohydrate, 5 Fat • **Carbohydrate Choices:** 2 1/2

High Altitude (3500 to 6500 feet): Use 10 × 1 1/2-inch pie plate. Use 1/4 cup Bisquick mix; add 1/4 cup all-purpose flour.

Impossibly Easy

Fudgy Chocolate–Pecan Pie

Prep: **15 min** Bake: **55 min** Cool: **1 hr**

8 servings

3 eggs

1/2 cup milk

1/4 cup butter or margarine, melted

4 ounces sweet baking chocolate, melted and cooled

1/2 cup packed brown sugar

1/2 cup Original Bisquick mix

1/2 cup granulated sugar

2/3 cup chopped pecans

1/2 cup pecan halves

Ice cream or Sweetened Whipped Cream (page 147), if desired

1 Heat oven to 350°. Spray pie plate, 9 × 1 1/4 inches, with cooking spray.

2 Place all ingredients except pecans and ice cream in blender. Cover and blend on high speed about 1 minute, stopping blender occasionally to scrape sides, until smooth. (Or beat in medium bowl with hand beater 2 minutes.) Stir in chopped pecans. Pour into pie plate. Arrange pecan halves on top.

3 Bake 50 to 55 minutes or until knife inserted in center comes out clean. Cool completely, about 1 hour. Serve with ice cream.

1 SERVING: Calories 415 (Calories from Fat 225); Fat 25g (Saturated 8g); Cholesterol 100mg; Sodium 190mg; Carbohydrate 42g (Dietary Fiber 2g); Protein 6g • % Daily Value: Vitamin A 8%; Vitamin C 0%; Calcium 8%; Iron 8% • **Exchanges:** 2 Starch, 1 Other Carbohydrate, 4 1/2 Fat • **Carbohydrate Choices:** 3

High Altitude (3500 to 6500 feet): Use 10 × 1 1/2-inch pie plate. Use 1/4 cup Bisquick mix; add 1/4 cup all-purpose flour.

Impossibly Easy
Pecan Pie

Prep: **10 min**   Bake: **55 min**   Stand: **5 min**

8 servings

1 1/2 cups chopped pecans

3/4 cup packed brown sugar

1/2 cup Original Bisquick mix

1/4 cup butter or margarine, melted

3/4 cup whipping (heavy) cream

3/4 cup light or dark corn syrup

1 1/2 teaspoons vanilla

4 eggs

Sweetened Whipped Cream (page 147), if desired

1 Heat oven to 350°. Spray pie plate, 9 × 1 1/4 inches, with cooking spray. Sprinkle pecans in pie plate.

2 Stir remaining ingredients except Sweetened Whipped Cream in medium bowl with wire whisk or fork until blended. Pour into pie plate.

3 Bake 50 to 55 minutes or until golden brown and knife inserted in center comes out clean. Let stand 5 minutes before serving. Serve with Sweetened Whipped Cream. Store covered in refrigerator.

Crowd-Size Impossibly Easy Pecan Pie: Double all ingredients. Spray 13 × 9 × 2-inch baking dish with cooking spray. Stir Bisquick mixture in large bowl. Bake 58 to 68 minutes or until knife inserted 2 inches from edge of dish comes out clean and top is deep golden brown (center may wiggle slightly).

1 SERVING: Calories 520 (Calories from Fat 290); Fat 32g (Saturated 10g); Cholesterol 145mg; Sodium 230mg; Carbohydrate 52g (Dietary Fiber 2g); Protein 6g • **% Daily Value:** Vitamin A 12%; Vitamin C 0%; Calcium 8%; Iron 8% • **Exchanges:** 1 Starch, 2 1/2 Other Carbohydrate, 6 1/2 Fat • **Carbohydrate Choices:** 3 1/2

High Altitude (3500 to 6500 feet): No changes.

Impossibly Easy

Butterscotch–Pecan Pie

Prep: **10 min**   Bake: **30 min**

8 servings

1 cup milk

1/4 cup butter or margarine, softened

1 teaspoon vanilla

2 eggs

1 cup packed brown sugar

1/2 cup Original Bisquick mix

1 cup chopped pecans

Sweetened Whipped Cream (below), if desired

1 Heat oven to 350°. Spray pie plate, 9 × 1 1/4 inches, with cooking spray.

2 Place all ingredients except pecans and Sweetened Whipped Cream in blender. Cover and blend on high speed about 1 minute or until smooth. (Or beat in medium bowl with electric mixer on high speed 2 minutes.) Pour into pie plate. Sprinkle with pecans.

3 Bake about 30 minutes or until set and knife inserted in center comes out clean. Serve warm or cold with Sweetened Whipped Cream. Store covered in refrigerator.

Sweetened Whipped Cream

1 cup whipping (heavy) cream

2 tablespoons powdered sugar

Beat ingredients in chilled small bowl with electric mixer on high speed until soft peaks form.

1 SERVING: Calories 430 (Calories from Fat 260); Fat 29g (Saturated 11g); Cholesterol 100mg; Sodium 200mg; Carbohydrate 38g (Dietary Fiber 2g); Protein 5g • % Daily Value: Vitamin A 14%; Vitamin C 0%; Calcium 10%; Iron 6% • Exchanges: 1 1/2 Starch, 1 Other Carbohydrate, 5 1/2 Fat • Carbohydrate Choices: 2 1/2

High Altitude (3500 to 6500 feet): Use 1/4 cup Bisquick mix; add 1/4 cup all-purpose flour. Bake 40 to 45 minutes.

Impossibly Easy
Maple-Nut Pie

Prep: **20 min** Bake: **40 min** Cool: **30 min**
Chill: **2 hr**

8 servings

1/2 cup coarsely chopped pecans or walnuts

1/2 cup Original Bisquick mix

1 cup milk

2 tablespoons butter or margarine, softened

1/2 teaspoon maple extract

2 eggs

1/3 cup packed brown sugar

1 package (3 ounces) cream cheese, cut into 9 pieces and softened

1/2 cup whipping (heavy) cream

2 tablespoons packed brown sugar

Pecan or walnut halves, if desired

1 Heat oven to 350°. Spray pie plate, 9 × 1 1/4 inches, with cooking spray. Sprinkle chopped pecans evenly in pie plate.

2 Place Bisquick mix, milk, butter, maple extract, eggs and 1/3 cup brown sugar in blender. Cover and blend on high speed 15 seconds or until smooth. Add cream cheese cubes one at a time, blending a few seconds after each addition. Blend 30 seconds longer or until smooth. Pour into pie plate.

3 Bake 35 to 40 minutes or until set and knife inserted in center comes out sticky but not wet. Cool 30 minutes. Refrigerate at least 2 hours until chilled.

4 Beat whipping cream and 2 tablespoons brown sugar in chilled small bowl with electric mixer on high speed until stiff peaks form; spoon onto pie. Arrange pecan halves on outside edge of whipped cream. Store covered in refrigerator.

1 SERVING: Calories 280 (Calories from Fat 180); Fat 20g (Saturated 9g); Cholesterol 90mg; Sodium 200mg; Carbohydrate 20g (Dietary Fiber 1g); Protein 5g • **% Daily Value:** Vitamin A 10%; Vitamin C 0%; Calcium 8%; Iron 4% • **Exchanges:** 1 Starch, 4 1/2 Fat • **Carbohydrate Choices:** 1

High Altitude (3500 to 6500 feet): No changes.

148

Impossibly Easy

Coconut Pie

Prep: **9 min** Bake: **55 min** Cool: **5 min**

8 servings

1 cup flaked or shredded coconut

3/4 cup sugar

1/2 cup Original Bisquick mix

1/4 cup butter or margarine, softened

2 cups milk

1 1/2 teaspoons vanilla

4 eggs

Whipped topping, if desired

Papaya or mango slices, if desired

1 Heat oven to 350°. Spray pie plate, 9 × 1 1/4 inches, with cooking spray.

2 Stir all ingredients except whipped topping and papaya in medium bowl with wire whisk or fork until blended. Pour into pie plate.

3 Bake 50 to 55 minutes or knife inserted in center comes out clean. Cool 5 minutes. Garnish with whipped topping and papaya. Store covered in refrigerator.

Reduced-Fat Impossibly Easy Coconut Pie: Use Reduced Fat Bisquick mix and fat-free (skim) milk. Substitute 6 egg whites or 1 cup fat-free cholesterol-free egg product for the eggs.

1 SERVING: Calories 270 (Calories from Fat 125); Fat 14g (Saturated 6g); Cholesterol 110mg; Sodium 270mg; Carbohydrate 31g (Dietary Fiber 1g); Protein 6g. • % **Daily Value:** Vitamin A 14%; Vitamin C 0%; Calcium 10%; Iron 4% • **Exchanges:** 1 Starch, 1 Other Carbohydrate, 3 Fat • **Carbohydrate Choices:** 2

High Altitude (3500 to 6500 feet): No changes.

Impossibly Easy
Sweet Buttermilk Pie

Prep: **5 min** Bake: **35 min** Cool: **5 min**

8 servings

1 1/2 cups sugar

1/2 cup Original Bisquick mix

1/3 cup butter or margarine, melted

1 cup buttermilk

1 teaspoon vanilla

3 eggs

1 Heat oven to 350°. Spray pie plate, 9 × 1 1/4 inches, with cooking spray.

2 Stir all ingredients in medium bowl with wire whisk or fork until blended. Pour into pie plate.

3 Bake 30 to 35 minutes or until knife inserted in center comes out clean. Cool 5 minutes. Store covered in refrigerator.

1 SERVING: Calories 290 (Calories from Fat 100); Fat 11g (Saturated 6g); Cholesterol 100mg; Sodium 210mg; Carbohydrate 43g (Dietary Fiber 0g); Protein 4g • **% Daily Value:** Vitamin A 8%; Vitamin C 0%; Calcium 6%; Iron 2% • **Exchanges:** 1 Starch, 2 Other Carbohydrate, 2 Fat • **Carbohydrate Choices:** 3

High Altitude (3500 to 6500 feet): Use 3/4 cup Bisquick mix. Bake 35 to 40 minutes.

Eggnog Pie

Prep: **10 min** Bake: **40 min** Cool: **5 min**

8 servings

1 1/2 cups eggnog

1/2 cup sugar

1/2 cup Original Bisquick mix

4 eggs

2 tablespoons rum or 1 teaspoon rum extract

Ground nutmeg

Nutmeg Whipped Cream (below), if desired

1 Heat oven to 350°. Spray pie plate, 9 × 1 1/4 inches, with cooking spray.

2 Place all ingredients except nutmeg and Nutmeg Whipped Cream in blender. Cover and blend on high speed 15 seconds. Pour into pie plate. Sprinkle with nutmeg.

3 Bake about 40 minutes or until knife inserted in center comes out clean. Cool 5 minutes. Serve warm or cold with Nutmeg Whipped Cream. Store covered in refrigerator.

Nutmeg Whipped Cream

1/2 cup whipping (heavy) cream

1 tablespoon sugar

1/4 teaspoon ground nutmeg

Beat all ingredients in chilled small bowl with electric mixer on high speed until soft peaks form.

1 SERVING: Calories 200 (Calories from Fat 90); Fat 10g (Saturated 5g); Cholesterol 160mg; Sodium 170mg; Carbohydrate 22g (Dietary Fiber 0g); Protein 6g • **% Daily Value:** Vitamin A 8%; Vitamin C 0%; Calcium 8%; Iron 4% • **Exchanges:** 1 Starch, 1/2 Milk, 2 Fat • **Carbohydrate Choices:** 1 1/2

High Altitude (3500 to 6500 feet): No changes.

HELPFUL NUTRITION AND
Cooking Information

NUTRITION GUIDELINES

We provide nutrition information for each recipe that includes calories, fat, cholesterol, sodium, carbohydrate, fiber and protein. Individual food choices can be based on this information.

Recommended intake for a daily diet of 2,000 calories as set by the Food and Drug Administration

Total Fat	Less than 65g
Saturated Fat	Less than 20g
Cholesterol	Less than 300mg
Sodium	Less than 2,400mg
Total Carbohydrate	300g
Dietary Fiber	25g

Criteria Used for Calculating Nutrition Information

- The first ingredient was used wherever a choice is given (such as 1/3 cup sour cream or plain yogurt).

- The first ingredient amount was used wherever a range is given (such as 3- to 3-1/2–pound cut-up broiler-fryer chicken).

- The first serving number was used wherever a range is given (such as 4 to 6 servings).

- "If desired" ingredients and recipe variations were not included (such as sprinkle with brown sugar, if desired).

- Only the amount of a marinade or frying oil that is estimated to be absorbed by the food during preparation or cooking was calculated.

Ingredients Used in Recipe Testing and Nutrition Calculations

- Ingredients used for testing represent those that the majority of consumers use in their homes: large eggs, 2% milk, 80%-lean ground beef, canned ready-to-use chicken broth and vegetable oil spread containing not less than 65 percent fat.

- Fat-free, low-fat or low-sodium products were not used, unless otherwise indicated.

- Solid vegetable shortening (not butter, margarine, nonstick cooking sprays or vegetable oil spread as they can cause sticking problems) was used to grease pans, unless otherwise indicated.

Equipment Used in Recipe Testing

We use equipment for testing that the majority of consumers use in their homes. If a specific piece of equipment (such as a wire whisk) is necessary for recipe success, it is listed in the recipe.

- Cookware and bakeware without nonstick coatings were used, unless otherwise indicated.

- No dark-colored, black or insulated bakeware was used.

- When a pan is specified in a recipe, a metal pan was used; a baking dish or pie plate means ovenproof glass was used.

- An electric hand mixer was used for mixing only when mixer speeds are specified in the recipe directions. When a mixer speed is not given, a spoon or fork was used.

Cooking Terms Glossary

Beat: Mix ingredients vigorously with spoon, fork, wire whisk, hand beater or electric mixer until smooth and uniform.

Boil: Heat liquid until bubbles rise continuously and break on the surface and steam is given off. For rolling boil, the bubbles form rapidly.

Chop: Cut into coarse or fine irregular pieces with a knife, food chopper, blender or food processor.

Cube: Cut into squares 1/2 inch or larger.

Dice: Cut into squares smaller than 1/2 inch.

Grate: Cut into tiny particles using small rough holes of grater (citrus peel or chocolate).

Grease: Rub the inside surface of a pan with shortening, using pastry brush, piece of waxed paper or paper towel, to prevent food from sticking during baking (as for some casseroles).

Julienne: Cut into thin, matchlike strips, using knife or food processor (vegetables, fruits, meats).

Mix: Combine ingredients in any way that distributes them evenly.

Sauté: Cook foods in hot oil or margarine over medium-high heat with frequent tossing and turning motion.

Shred: Cut into long thin pieces by rubbing food across the holes of a shredder, as for cheese, or by using a knife to slice very thinly, as for cabbage.

Simmer: Cook in liquid just below the boiling point on top of the stove; usually after reducing heat from a boil. Bubbles will rise slowly and break just below the surface.

Stir: Mix ingredients until uniform consistency. Stir once in a while for stirring occasionally, often for stirring frequently and continuously for stirring constantly.

Toss: Tumble ingredients (such as green salad) lightly with a lifting motion, usually to coat evenly or mix with another food.

Metric Conversion Guide

Volume

U.S. Units	Canadian Metric	Australian Metric
1/4 teaspoon	1 mL	1 ml
1/2 teaspoon	2 mL	2 ml
1 teaspoon	5 mL	5 ml
1 tablespoon	15 mL	20 ml
1/4 cup	50 mL	60 ml
1/3 cup	75 mL	80 ml
1/2 cup	125 mL	125 ml
2/3 cup	150 mL	170 ml
3/4 cup	175 mL	190 ml
1 cup	250 mL	250 ml
1 quart	1 liter	1 liter
1 1/2 quarts	1.5 liters	1.5 liters
2 quarts	2 liters	2 liters
2 1/2 quarts	2.5 liters	2.5 liters
3 quarts	3 liters	3 liters
4 quarts	4 liters	4 liters

Weight

U.S. Units	Canadian Metric	Australian Metric
1 ounce	30 grams	30 grams
2 ounces	55 grams	60 grams
3 ounces	85 grams	90 grams
4 ounces (1/4 pound)	115 grams	125 grams
8 ounces (1/2 pound)	225 grams	225 grams
16 ounces (1 pound)	455 grams	500 grams
1 pound	455 grams	1/2 kilogram

Measurements

Inches	Centimeters
1	2.5
2	5.0
3	7.5
4	10.0
5	12.5
6	15.0
7	17.5
8	20.5
9	23.0
10	25.5
11	28.0
12	30.5
13	33.0

Temperatures

Fahrenheit	Celsius
32°	0°
212°	100°
250°	120°
275°	140°
300°	150°
325°	160°
350°	180°
375°	190°
400°	200°
425°	220°
450°	230°
475°	240°
500°	260°

Note: The recipes in this cookbook have not been developed or tested using metric measures. When converting recipes to metric, some variations in quality may be noted.

Index

Complete your cookbook library with these *Betty Crocker* titles

Betty Crocker Baking for Today
Betty Crocker Basics
Betty Crocker's Best Bread Machine Cookbook
Betty Crocker's Best Chicken Cookbook
Betty Crocker's Best Christmas Cookbook
Betty Crocker's Best of Baking
Betty Crocker's Best of Healthy and Hearty Cooking
Betty Crocker's Best-Loved Recipes
Betty Crocker's Bisquick® Cookbook
Betty Crocker Bisquick® II Cookbook
Betty Crocker Bisquick® Impossibly Easy Pies
Betty Crocker Celebrate!
Betty Crocker's Complete Thanksgiving Cookbook
Betty Crocker's Cook Book for Boys and Girls
Betty Crocker's Cook It Quick
Betty Crocker Cookbook, 10th Edition— *The* **BIG RED** *Cookbook*®
Betty Crocker's Cookbook, Bridal Edition
Betty Crocker's Cookie Book
Betty Crocker's Cooking Basics
Betty Crocker's Cooking for Two
Betty Crocker's Cooky Book, Facsimile Edition
Betty Crocker's Diabetes Cookbook
Betty Crocker Dinner Made Easy with Rotisserie Chicken
Betty Crocker Easy Family Dinners
Betty Crocker's Easy Slow Cooker Dinners
Betty Crocker's Eat and Lose Weight
Betty Crocker's Entertaining Basics
Betty Crocker's Flavors of Home
Betty Crocker 4-Ingredient Dinners
Betty Crocker Grilling Made Easy
Betty Crocker Healthy Heart Cookbook
Betty Crocker's Healthy New Choices
Betty Crocker's Indian Home Cooking
Betty Crocker's Italian Cooking
Betty Crocker's Kids Cook!
Betty Crocker's Kitchen Library
Betty Crocker's Living with Cancer Cookbook
Betty Crocker Low-Carb Lifestyle Cookbook
Betty Crocker's Low-Fat, Low-Cholesterol Cooking Today
Betty Crocker More Slow Cooker Recipes
Betty Crocker's New Cake Decorating
Betty Crocker's New Chinese Cookbook
Betty Crocker One-Dish Meals
Betty Crocker's A Passion for Pasta
Betty Crocker's Picture Cook Book, Facsimile Edition
Betty Crocker's Quick & Easy Cookbook
Betty Crocker's Slow Cooker Cookbook
Betty Crocker's Ultimate Cake Mix Cookbook
Betty Crocker's Vegetarian Cookbook